Hiking Central Florida

For Jeff, Carolyn, and David Butler.
Sharing the outdoors with you for so many years
was always the best part of living in Central Florida.

Hiking
Central Florida

A Guide to the Area's Greatest Hiking Adventures

Second Edition

M. Timothy O'Keefe

ESSEX, CONNECTICUT

FALCONGUIDES®

An imprint of The Globe Pequot Publishing Group, Inc.
64 South Main Street
Essex, CT 06426
www.globepequot.com

Falcon and FalconGuides are registered trademarks and Make Adventure Your Story is a trademark of The Rowman & Littlefield Publishing Group, Inc.

Distributed by NATIONAL BOOK NETWORK

British Library Cataloguing in Publication Information available

Library of Congress Cataloging-in-Publication Data

Names: O'Keefe, M. Timothy, author.
Title: Hiking central Florida : a guide to the area's greatest hiking adventures / M. Timothy O'Keefe.
Description: Second edition. | Essex, Connecticut : FalconGuides, 2024. |
Summary: "Hiking Central Florida describes forty hikes designed to highlight some of the best natural areas throughout the region"—Provided by publisher.
Identifiers: LCCN 2024002909 (print) | LCCN 2024002910 (ebook) | ISBN 9781493080045 (paperback) | ISBN 9781493080052 (epub)
Subjects: LCSH: Hiking—Florida—Guidebooks. | Trails—Florida—Guidebooks. | Florida—Guidebooks.
Classification: LCC GV199.42.F6 O54 2024 (print) | LCC GV199.42.F6 (ebook) | DDC 796.5109759—dc23/eng/20240213
LC record available at https://lccn.loc.gov/2024002909
LC ebook record available at https://lccn.loc.gov/2024002910

Contents

The Hikes

SHORT FAMILY HIKES

DAY HIKES

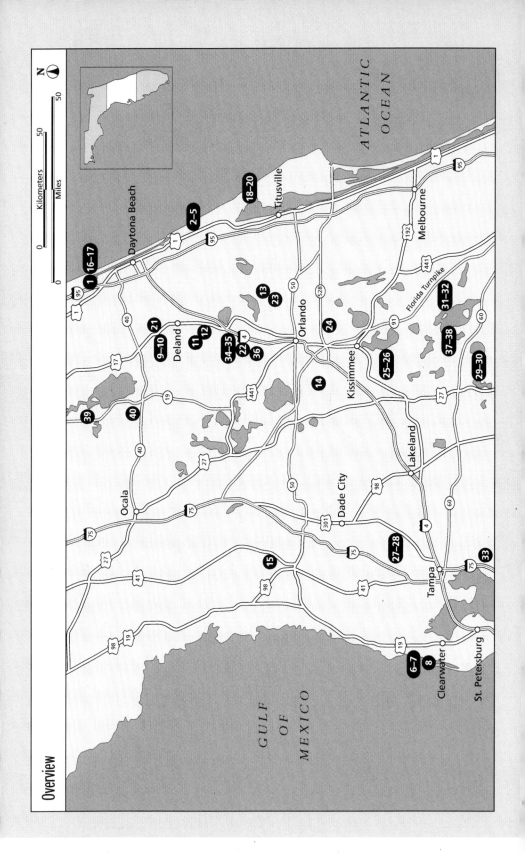

Overview

Acknowledgments

A guidebook to Central Florida hiking is possible only because of the untiring efforts of the Florida Trail Association (FTA). This volunteer organization was responsible first for creating and now for maintaining many of the state's best wilderness hiking trails, particularly the Florida National Scenic Trail (also known as the Florida Trail, FT and FNST).

Also responsible for opening up and conserving hundreds of miles of Central Florida pathways are staffs and volunteer helpers of the Florida Department of Agriculture and Consumer Services, Florida Department of Environmental Services, Florida Fish and Wildlife Conservation Commission, the US National Park Service, USDA Forest Service, and the US Fish and Wildlife Service. They administer the state parks, the state and national forests, and the state and national wildlife refuges, wildlife management areas, and preserves.

They are the people who make hiking on public lands possible. After every hurricane, they have a tremendous cleanup workload and always do a terrific job.

Meet Your Guide

M. Timothy O'Keefe authored the first hiking book for the entire state of Florida: *The Hiker's Guide to Florida*, published by Falcon Press. Retitled *Hiking Florida* since the second edition, it has generated three regional guides: *Hiking Central Florida, Hiking North Florida and the Panhandle, and Hiking South Florida and the Keys.*

Tim's other books are *The Photographer's Guide to the Everglades, Caribbean Hiking, The Spicy Camp Cook Book, Seasonal Guide to the Natural Year: Florida with Georgia and Alabama Coasts, Great Adventures in Florida, Manatees: Our Vanishing Mermaids, Sea Turtles: The Watcher's Guide, Fish and Dive the Caribbean* and *Fish and Dive Florida & The Keys* (both with Larry Larsen), *Diving to Adventure,* and *AAA's A Photo Journey to Central Florida,* published by the American Automobile Association.

A longtime freelance writer and photographer, his photographs have been published online and in numerous national and international print publications more than 15,000 times. Tim's work has won more than fifty regional and national awards. *The Spicy Camp Cook Book* and *Seasonal Guide to the Natural Year: Florida with Georgia and Alabama Coasts* were named "Best Book" by the Florida Outdoor Writers Association.

Tim received a PhD from the University of North Carolina at Chapel Hill. Before retiring to freelance full-time, Tim was a professor and head of the journalism division in the Nicholson School of Communication and Media at the University of Central Florida, where he founded the Journalism program.

Introduction

No mountain high enough, no valley low enough. . . . What Central Florida hiking is like.

Central Florida Overview

Central Florida hiking is some of the easiest in all of North America. Florida, essentially a spit of sand between the Gulf of Mexico and the Atlantic Ocean, is an exceedingly flat place. You'll find no mountains to climb, no deep valleys to descend, no dangerous precipices to teeter on.

Rolling hills do break up the flat landscape in a few places, but those mounds are hardly formidable. Britton Hill, the highest elevation in Florida, is just 345 feet above sea level. Located near the town of Lakewood Park in the Florida Panhandle, it is the lowest high point of any state in the country.

Our geographic definition of Central Florida extends from Ocala National Forest to SR 60 near Lake Wales and Yeehaw Junction. Almost all of the forty Central Florida trails described here are true hiking experiences on trails not shared with cyclists, skateboarders, or horses, whose residual presence is not always appreciated in our hot Florida climate.

The hikes in this guide are designed to highlight some of the best natural areas and historical sites throughout the region. They fall into four categories: Short Family Hikes, ranging from 1 to 3 miles; Day Hikes, from 4 to 12 miles; Overnight Hikes, with an easy walk to a primitive campsite; and Long Haulers, true backpacking experiences that may require a weekend or more to complete. For other parts of Florida, check out my other regional books: *Hiking South Florida and the Keys* and *Hiking North Florida and the Panhandle.*

Central Florida hiking is within the capabilities of almost everyone, from the youngest walkers to the oldest. During the driest months—January to mid-May—when the ground is hard, many trails are barrier free. Boardwalk nature trails at many state parks are well suited for wheelchairs year-round. In addition to wilderness paths, you'll find mile after mile of beautiful beaches, some of the best in the nation. Several of these exceptional beaches are located in Florida state parks and the National Park System.

Florida's most striking landscape is located at sea level and also underground. In addition to its many famous beaches, the state has more than 1,000 freshwater springs, more than 7,500 lakes, and almost 1,700 rivers and streams. Numerous freshwater caves are hidden underground.

Most of these springs and lakes were carved from the state's limestone landscape, known as karst. During the estimated 100 to 300 million years Florida was covered by the sea, limestone and shells and other marine deposits accumulated to form the state's crust. The layer of fossilized plant and animals varies from hundreds to thousands of feet thick beneath most of Florida. This limestone bedrock, known as the Florida Platform, is continuously reshaped by both rain and groundwater erosion.

Over time, the large hollows, caves, and fissures created by erosion cause the ground surface to occasionally collapse, creating a sinkhole or a craterlike depression. Since this wearing away never ceases, new sinkholes may appear at any time. The sand now covering much of inland Florida was created over millions of years by wave action breaking apart the bedrock near or just above the surface.

Central Florida Weather

Florida is nicknamed the Sunshine State, and its summers are hot, sunny, and humid due to its rainy season. Central Florida's climate is classified as humid subtropical. It may not seem logical, but a subtropical area has hotter summers than tropical zones. And although summer in every region of Florida may seem similar, winter in the subtropical region is often considerably colder.

Summer is the prime hiking season in most of the country—but not in Florida. November to May has the best hiking weather. Humidity and heat make the summer outdoors too uncomfortable for many.

Higher humidity usually begins in May. Although the National Weather Service defines the Central Florida rainy season as the period between May 25 and October 10, frequent rains may begin in April and extend into November. When a tropical storm visits, it may dump as much as 10 to 30 inches of water on a region.

Caution: After any tropical storm or hurricane event, no hiking plans should be made for an impacted area without thoroughly checking on the status of the trails you want to hike. Minor damage may be repaired over a period of six to nine months, but sometimes it takes years to put a trail back in shape.

As the humidity increases with rainy season, air temperatures also go higher. From June until late September, they are routinely in the 90°F to 100°F-plus range. Days of 100°F-plus once were rare, but they have become more common as the climate warms. The early morning is the only time to hike comfortably in summer. Even in October and November, temperatures may be 90°F and above.

The best way to gauge how hot it feels outside is with the Heat Index. Using the chart on page 3, you can measure the amount of heat stress you may experience with the dew point, which measures how much water vapor is in the atmosphere. How comfortable you feel on a hot day is determined by both the humidity level and the air temperature.

How do you find the dew point? It's easy. You could simply ask, "Hey Siri/Alexa, what's the dew point?" Or look at your cell phone's weather app and scroll through the day's statistics. You should find a "Feels Like" temperature or Heat Index for your location.

Unfortunately, the Heat Index is not entirely accurate. It is based on the temperature measured in the *shade*, not in the *sun*. Why do meteorologists determine a day's official high temperature from a shaded thermometer? They say the temperature in the shade is closest to the actual air temperature.

They also agree that it does feel hotter in the sun because the sun's radiation does cause a higher temperature. Measuring the temperature in the sun would heat the liquid in the thermometer, causing the reading to be higher than the true air temperature.

Well, as we humans contain more than 50 percent water, we can relate to the sun's impact on a thermometer. And on us.

The National Weather Service (NWS) admits its thermometer-in-the-shade approach has flaws, stating: "If you are exposed to direct sunlight, the Heat Index value can be increased by up to 15°F" (weather.gov/ama/heatindex).

Hikers in Central Florida don't always have lots of shade. So consider adding as much as 15°F to the temperature when you plan a summer hike.

As the NWS also points out, "heat indices meeting or exceeding 103°F can lead to dangerous heat disorders with prolonged exposure and/or physical activity in the heat."

Although the Heat Index ignores the sun's radiant heat, it is the standard for measuring outdoor conditions. It's up to you to add 5 to 15 degrees to judge the heat outside. Or set a thermometer in a sunny area.

Heat Index Chart (Temperature & Dewpoint)

Dewpoint (°F)	Temperature (°F)															
	90	91	92	93	94	95	96	97	98	99	100	101	102	103	104	105
65	94	95	96	97	98	100	101	102	103	104	106	107	108	109	110	112
66	94	95	97	98	99	100	101	103	104	105	106	108	109	110	111	112
67	95	96	97	98	100	101	102	103	105	106	107	108	110	111	112	113
68	95	97	98	99	100	102	103	104	105	107	108	109	110	112	113	114
69	96	97	99	100	101	103	104	105	106	108	109	110	111	113	114	115
70	97	98	99	101	102	103	105	106	107	109	110	111	112	114	115	116
71	98	99	100	102	103	104	106	107	108	109	111	112	113	115	116	117
72	98	100	101	103	104	105	107	108	109	111	112	113	114	116	117	118
73	99	101	102	103	105	106	108	109	110	112	113	114	116	117	118	119
74	100	102	103	104	106	107	109	110	111	113	114	115	117	118	119	121
75	101	103	104	106	107	108	110	111	113	114	115	117	118	119	121	122
76	102	104	105	107	108	110	111	112	114	115	117	118	119	121	122	123
77	103	105	106	108	109	111	112	114	115	117	118	119	121	122	124	125
78	105	106	108	109	111	112	114	115	117	118	119	121	122	124	125	126
79	106	107	109	111	112	114	115	117	118	120	121	122	124	125	127	128
80	107	109	110	112	114	115	117	118	120	121	123	124	126	127	128	130
81	109	110	112	114	115	117	118	120	121	123	124	126	127	129	130	132
82	110	112	114	115	117	118	120	122	123	125	126	128	129	131	132	133

Note: *Exposure to full sunshine can increase HI values by up to 15° F*

Central Florida's summer humidity often falls into the 60 to 80 percent range, which is why locals may limit their outdoor summer activity. Since so few people hike from May to October, the Florida Trail Association normally does not perform trail maintenance in those months.

Other aspects of Florida weather, such as lightning, hurricanes, sun exposure, and hypothermia, are covered in the next chapter, "Before You Hit the Trail," under "Safety."

Florida's Native American Tribes

Little is known about Florida's first native inhabitants. They date back 12,000 to 15,000 years ago, and artifacts from that period are sparse due to both Florida's acidic soil and the rise in sea level. Since the first Native Americans settled in Florida, the sea has risen about 300 feet, covering many of the early settlements and ceremonial mounds, some now located as far as 20 miles into the Gulf.

Almost all Native American objects that have been found are stone tools, knives, arrowheads, and scrapers. However, canoes dating back 5,000 and 6,000 years were discovered in two Central Florida springs, leaving the possibility of other major finds.

Perhaps 1,500 years ago, Florida had more than a dozen identifiable Native American tribes. The two largest groups were the Timucua and the Calusa. The Timucua lived in North Florida and parts of Central Florida and maintained a loose alliance with tribes sharing the same language and traditions. The Calusa and tribes associated with them controlled much of South Florida. A number of smaller groups lived in the Tampa Bay area.

An estimated 200,000 Native Americans lived in Florida when the Spanish arrived in 1513. They were not interested in establishing friendly relations with the foreigners. The natives not only resisted, they devastated almost every Spanish expedition between 1513 and 1568. That included the famous visit by explorer Juan Ponce de León, who gave Florida its name. He died from an infection after being hit by a Calusa arrow.

However, by 1800 the diseases introduced by the Spanish coupled with Spanish brutality effectively destroyed Florida's Native American people. None of the original tribes still exist.

It's been said that everyone living in Florida is from somewhere else, and it's true. Beginning around 1770, new groups of Native Americans began moving to Florida from Georgia, Alabama, and several other nearby states. The Spanish called these newcomers *cimarrones*, "wild runaways." Joining the Native Americans were runaway slaves and even Europeans. By the end of the 1700s, this diverse collection of people became known as the Seminoles.

The Seminole Tribe of Florida

The Seminoles moved to Florida seeking a place to live and avoid conflict with English settlers wanting their land. As it turned out, the US government wanted all the land for itself. Although the United States didn't acquire Florida from Spain until 1819, the First Seminole War took place from 1817 to 1818, when the US military invaded Spanish Florida to punish the Seminoles for hiding escaped slaves. The army succeeded in pushing the Seminoles farther south.

Once the United States owned Florida, the federal government implemented the 1830 Indian Removal Act in an attempt to send the Seminoles to Oklahoma. Some refused to be deported, resulting in the Second Seminole War (1835–1842), in which an estimated 3,000 Seminole warriors faced off against more than 30,000 US troops.

The Seminoles waged a guerilla campaign that killed between 1,500 and 2,000 soldiers and an unknown number of civilians. Hostilities unofficially ended in June 1842, although no treaty was ever signed. The Second Seminole War was the longest and most expensive war waged against Native Americans. The unresolved conflict cost the US government an estimated $20 million.

The Third Seminole War (1855–1858), the last Indian war battled east of the Mississippi, was fought over land conflicts between the Seminole residents and arriving settlers. Rewards paid for captured Seminoles and military skirmishes left only about 300 Seminoles remaining when the dispute ended. The survivors retreated into the Everglades, a territory no one wanted. The Florida Seminoles finally were left alone, and they stayed at peace.

Of all the Native Americans in the United States, the Florida Seminoles are the only ones who never surrendered and never signed a peace treaty. As a result, the Seminoles proudly call themselves the "Unconquered People."

After the Third Seminole War, Florida's Seminoles were determined to stay free. Although few in numbers, their proud spirit was strong. They wanted absolutely no interference from the outside, from non-Indians. To that end, their leaders forbade formal schooling until well into the twentieth century. Christianity was also held at bay until the 1930s.

The Seminoles lived mostly in poverty until 1979. But in that year the tribe defied state and federal laws by opening its first casino on its own land. This sparked what has become a multibillion-dollar industry for the Seminoles and other tribes nationwide. Today the Seminole Tribe owns six casinos, whose gaming activities are still counter to Florida law. State law, however, does not govern sovereign Indian lands. The Seminoles are a federally recognized sovereign nation that cannot be sued.

The casino business quickly changed the tribe's finances. To the surprise of many, in 2006 the Seminole Tribe made a $965 million purchase of the Hard Rock International hotel, cafe, and casino chain, which today operates in more than seventy-four countries. The hospitality and gambling businesses place the tribe's net worth beyond $12 billion. The world's largest Hard Rock Cafe is in Central Florida at Universal

Seminole women in South Florida wearing patchwork clothing

Studios Orlando. The Seminole Tribe's largest casino is the Seminole Hard Rock Hotel & Casino Tampa, also in Central Florida.

As of 2019, more than 4,000 members of the Seminole Tribe of Florida were living on six reservations in Florida.

The Miccosukee Tribe of Indians of Florida

Florida's other Native American tribe is the Miccosukee, the descendants of the Creek Nation who migrated to Florida between 1767 and 1821. The Miccosukee remained with the Seminoles until 1957.

Once the Seminole Tribe of Florida was officially recognized by the US government as a nation in 1957, the Miccosukee identified their cultural differences with the Seminoles. They decided to become separate and established their own recognized and sovereign entity, the Miccosukee Tribe of Indians of Florida.

The Miccosukee Tribe has almost 600 members living on three sections of the Miccosukee Indian Reservation, located west of Miami and Fort Lauderdale.

Florida Flora and Fauna

Landscapes in Florida typically are classified according to the dominant biological communities and the animals living in them. These are usually broken down into the following categories. Hike descriptions often use these same terms in describing an area's topography.

Forest swamps: Also known as floodplain forest, these swamps are wet only part of the year. They are dominated by hardwoods such as water oak, black gum, sweet gum, and water hickory, with bald cypress and cabbage palm usually mixed in. Floodplain animals include bobcats, turkeys, deer, squirrels, otters, snakes, ducks, and songbirds.

Hammocks: In Florida, the term "hammock" applies to any significant grouping of broad-leaved trees. Prime examples are the live oak, cabbage palm, hickory, and sweetgum hammocks of Central Florida. The name hammock comes from an Indian word meaning "shady place." All hammocks generally enjoy fertile soil, and the trees remain green year-round. Animals commonly living in them are toads, flying squirrels, wood rats, and birds such as the flycatcher. Large animals such as Florida black bears and bobcats also live in hammocks.

Salt marshes: Usually found along the coasts, salt marshes can be mixed in with mangroves or exist as a separate community. Black rush and cordgrass are the dominant plants. When a salt marsh extends into tidal rivers, it often merges with freshwater marshes to form a fertile transition zone. Saltwater marshes are typically rich in bird and animal life, including otters, raccoons, turtles, snakes—and mosquitoes.

Freshwater marshes: A blend of sedge, grass, and rush, freshwater marshes have standing water for two or more months out of the year. Land with a shorter period of standing water is classified as a wet prairie. Freshwater marshes often house many endangered species. Look for wood storks, sandhill cranes, and Everglades kites. Alligators, waterfowl and wading birds, frogs, turtles, snakes, and otters also thrive in these marshes.

Dry prairies: These treeless plains contain grasses and saw palmetto, with live oak and cabbage palm hammocks and domes of cypress trees occasionally populating the flat spaces. A dry prairie may seem a lifeless, barren place, but closer inspection may reveal a considerable number of animals. Look for burrowing owls, sandhill cranes, raccoons, and bobcats.

Pine flatwoods: Pine flatwoods are the most common type of biological community in Florida, with three types of pine forests: pond pines growing in wet conditions, longleaf pines in the higher and drier regions, and slash pines in the transition zone between the two. Although each forest type is dominated by its particular pine species, animals such as Florida black bears, deer, bobcats, raccoons, gray foxes, squirrels, birds, and black snakes roam them all.

Sandhill areas: Fire is common in these dry and sparsely populated regions due to the arid conditions. It sometimes eliminates the longleaf pines, which are then supplanted by turkey and red oaks. Animals that burrow to avoid heat—and to escape the frequent fires—are common here. They include gopher tortoises, indigo snakes, and pocket gophers. In old-growth forest communities, you may be fortunate enough to spot an endangered red-cockaded woodpecker.

Wilderness Restrictions and Regulations

Note: All entry and other fees were accurate as of publication date. Check the respective properties for updates.

The Florida Department of Environmental Protection's Division of State Lands (DEP) is Florida's lead agency for environmental management and stewardship. It provides oversight for the management of activities on more than 12 million acres of public lands, including lakes, rivers, and islands. Different agencies under the DEP have their own set of rules and regulations. They all prohibit fireworks due to the risk of fire. Drones also are generally prohibited.

Canaveral National Seashore

The Canaveral National Seashore address is 7611 South Atlantic Ave., New Smyrna Beach 32169; (386) 428-3384; nps.gov/cana/contacts.htm.

Canaveral bans glass containers everywhere, pets on the beach, metal detectors, and any tampering or collecting of plant or animal species. Visitors must remove their litter from the seashore area and also place it in proper containers. Fires are limited to designated areas. Alcohol consumption is allowed subject to state law provisions. The drinking age in Florida is 21, no exceptions. Full Canaveral National Seashore regulations are available at nps.gov/cana/learn/management/lawsandpolicies.htm.

Failure to follow the Canaveral National Seashore regulations is expensive.

Florida Fish and Wildlife Conservation Commission

The Florida Fish and Wildlife Conservation Commission (FWC) enforces hunting and fishing laws. Many camping areas are located near lakes and shorelines. A fishing license is required for fresh water or salt water; a combination license includes both. Licenses are available online at GoOutdoorsFlorida.com, in person at a license agent or tax collector's office, or by calling toll-free (888) FISH-FLORIDA (888-347-4356). More information on freshwater fishing is available at https://myfwc.com/license/recreational/freshwater-fishing/.

Floridians who want to fish from a beach or shoreline are required to have a no-cost resident recreational saltwater shoreline fishing license (888-347-4356). Nonresidents wanting to fish must have a three-day, seven-day, or annual saltwater fishing license. For more information visit https://myfwc.com/license/recreational/saltwater-fishing/shoreline-faqs/. A fishing license from a visitor's home state is not valid in Florida. Georgians have limited exceptions but also certain restrictions.

Florida State Parks

Florida state parks attract numerous hikers to their campgrounds and trails. Located from Northwest Florida to the Keys, the parks are convenient for overnight and longer stays. Check the website of the park you want to visit for its particular rules: floridastateparks.org.

Banned inside all state parks are drones and the collection, destruction, and disturbance of plants and animals. Pets are allowed in some but not all parks. Where allowed, dogs must remain on a 6-foot handheld leash. They are not allowed on park beaches and concessionaire property. Service animals are allowed in all state parks. The pet policy is covered in detail at floridastateparks.org/PetPolicy.

Fires are limited to designated areas only. Campers are allowed to consume alcohol only within their campsite. Where allowed, primitive camping costs $5 per person per night. Details on making campground reservations are in the "Camping" section under "Wilderness Ethics" in the next chapter. All park rules can be found at florida stateparks.org/Rules.

Florida State Forests

Florida's state forests currently oversee thirty-eight forests and 1 ranch—a total of 1,167,787 acres. Links to all the state forests are available at fdacs.gov/Forest-Wildfire/Our-Forests/State-Forests.

The state forest $2 day-use pass must be purchased online in advance at florida stateforests.reserveamerica.com/posProducts.do?contractCode=FLFS. The speed limit on state forest roads is 30 miles per hour. In recreations areas and campgrounds, the speed limit is 10 miles per hour. Metal detectors and fireworks are banned. Glass bottles are banned around lakes and waterways.

Where allowed, pets must be on a leash 10 feet or shorter. Even if leashed, pets are not allowed around swimming areas. Always be certain your vehicle does not obstruct roads, gates, or fire lines. When leaving the forest, take all garbage with you when an empty trash container is not available.

Alcoholic beverages cannot be possessed or consumed in areas where they are posted as prohibited. Rope swings or diving from stream banks or trees is not allowed. Removal or destruction of cultural artifacts and plants is prohibited. To fish, you need a valid Florida fishing license.

Florida Wildlife Management Areas

Wildlife management areas (WMAs) have a day-use fee of $3 unless you have an Annual Management Area Permit costing $26.50. Day-use permits may be available at WMA entrance fee stations. Have the exact cash amount, since you will need to make a deposit at the fee station. Show the hangtag from the envelope on your vehicle when you go hiking. For more information visit myfwc.com/hunting/wma -brochures/. Fee collection is likely to go online in the future.

Ocala National Forest

Black bear interactions with people have become so common that Ocala National Forest *requires the use of approved bear-proof canisters* to store food. So-called "attractants" that appeal to bears must also be placed in canisters or a hardtop vehicle. Information on this Bear Aware program is available at fs.usda.gov/detail/florida/ learning?cid=fsbdev3_008653. Pay special attention to the list of attractants that must be placed in a bear-proof container. A single canister may not be large enough.

Leashed dogs are allowed on the Florida Trail sections with a natural surface but not on boardwalks. Special care is required with campfires, which may be prohibited during dry season. You are responsible for keeping your fire under control. Your fire should never be left unattended; most of all, make certain it is completely out before leaving your campsite.

Alerts and notices are posted at fs.usda.gov/alerts/florida/alerts-notices and should be checked before finalizing any plans. Information on a wide range of Ocala activities is available at fs.usda.gov/recarea/florida/recarea/?recid=83528.

The district ranger offices are open weekdays only from 7:30 a.m. to 4:30 p.m.; closed on weekends and federal holidays: Seminole Ranger District, 40929 State Road 19, Umatilla 32784; call (352) 669-3153. Lake George Ranger District, 17147 East State Road 40, Silver Springs 34488; call (352) 625-2520.

Accessibility

Some places have more accessibility options than others. Terrain, wildlife concerns, and an agency's purpose usually determine a location's accessibility.

Canaveral National Seashore

Made up mostly of sand, forest, and wetlands, the national seashore has only a few accessible features. The boardwalks leading to Playalinda and Apollo Beaches all start from the parking lot at ground level. Some boardwalks are fairly flat; others have inclines going over a sand dune. The restrooms and visitor center at Apollo Beach are accessible. Some of the trails located in the Apollo Beach section also are accessible. A loaner wheelchair is also available at Apollo Beach. No accessible camping is available.

Due to the region's sandy soil, accessible hikes are uncommon in much of Central Florida. Boardwalk hikes are the exception. They are almost always accessible.

Florida State Parks

Florida's state parks offer new and renovated buildings and facilities complying with accessible design standards. The parks offer many accessible camping areas, bathhouses, restrooms, recreation halls, environmental education centers, picnic pavilions, and more. Wheelchairs and manually powered mobility devices are permitted anywhere foot traffic is allowed. However, not every land area, such as beaches and muddy terrain, is suitable for these devices. Power-driven mobility devices may be used only by those with true mobility disabilities. Specifications for other power-driven mobility device (OPDMDs) are found at floridastateparks.org/wheelchairopdmd-policy.

Service animals are defined as "dogs that are individually trained to do work or perform tasks for people with genuine disabilities," according to the Revised Americans with Disabilities Act Service Animal Requirements. Service animals in a working capacity are allowed in all park public areas when accompanied by a visitor with a disability. The animals generally must be kept leashed or tethered. More information is available at: floridastateparks.org/PetPolicy.

Florida State Forests

Accessible facilities in Florida state forests tend to be less elaborate than those at Florida state parks. Although recreation is an important feature, the primary purposes

Because the Central Florida outdoors is popular with both locals and tourists, showing up without a campsite reservation is a risky move.

of the state forests is to maintain the forests' biological diversity, manage timber and wildlife habitat, and also protect Floridians from the dangers of wildland fire.

The state forest accessibility policy is to "provide persons with disabilities the highest feasible level of physical access to pedestrian trail facilities that is reasonable and consistent with the protection of natural and cultural resources and the outdoor recreational experiences of all visitors." Paths in undeveloped areas are left in their natural state.

Restrictions for the use of OPDMDs are spelled out at fdacs.gov/Forest -Wildfire/Our-Forests/State-Forests/State-Forest-Recreation/Use-of-Mobility -Devices-on-State-Forests.

The forest service suggests calling before visiting a location to determine if a particular OPDMD meets their criteria.

Florida Wildlife Management Areas

The Florida Fish and Wildlife Conservation Commission oversees these locations. Some hunting, fishing, and other recreational opportunities for persons with disabilities are available. Unfortunately, at the moment none of these are listed online according to location. Information about these opportunities, as well as permit applications to request the established accommodation and an AMP, can be found at https:// myfwc.com/license/accessibility/.

Ocala National Forest

Ocala National Forest is managed by the US Department of Agriculture. Its accessibility policy is to make its electronic and information technologies accessible to individuals with disabilities in a manner comparable to those who do not have disabilities, as required by law. It has two accessible locations. The seasonal Big Bass Campground is used mostly in hunting season (fs.usda.gov/recarea/florida/recreation/recarea/?recid=83716&actid=29). The Juniper Springs Recreation Area has the 0.4-mile-long Juniper Run Nature Trail, an accessible boardwalk.

The Benefits of Boardwalks

Although not usually regarded as a traditional hiking path, boardwalks do fulfill that function in Florida, so don't bypass them just because they're short. Florida is a wet place, and sometimes the best wildlife viewing is not on the dry uplands but in the interiors of cypress swamps. And they are usually accessible.

Cypress swamps are forbidding places that few people are willing to slog through and possibly encounter alligators and snakes. Yet white-tailed deer, Florida black bears, raccoons, otters, turtles, bobcats, and myriad birds make swamps their homes. Swamps are amazingly rich in birdlife, including wood storks, bald eagles, herons, and egrets. Swamps are where you find air plants and orchids.

A boardwalk is the best way to explore swamp interiors. Due to their construction cost, most boardwalks are fairly short, perhaps only 100 yards, although they can be considerably longer. You'll sometimes see more wildlife on a short boardwalk than on a mile of woodland hiking.

BEFORE YOU HIT THE TRAIL

Note: All prices were accurate as of publication date. Check the respective properties for updates.

Wilderness Ethics

Florida's warm weather and sunshine are the main reasons so many people move to the Sunshine State at the somewhat frightening rate of more than 1,000 people each day. World-class beaches and theme parks attract tourists from all over, making Florida one of the world's top tourist destinations.

The result of all this attention: Central Florida is in danger of being loved to death. As more and more land is developed into sites for homes, schools, and shopping malls, the forests and preserves become ever more precious. Florida officials are attempting to buy up and protect as much land as possible, but their funding will never match those of land developers.

It is up to us, the present-day users, to serve as stewards of the parks and preserves to ensure that our children and grandchildren have the same hiking opportunities. Although Central Florida may become ever more crowded, large sections of wilderness land should always endure.

How you can help:

- Always stay on the designated trails.
- Leave wildflowers, air plants, and other foliage where you find them.

When someone is attacked by an alligator (rare!), it's probably because people have been feeding the animal. The gator has lost its natural fear of humans and come to associate them with food.

- Never walk on sand dunes.
- Camp only in designated areas.
- Be vigilant with campfires.
- Be careful of human waste. Bury it at least 6 inches deep, a minimum of 200 feet from any water and 100 feet from any campsite.
- Wash dishes at least 200 feet from streams and lakes.
- Don't leave unwanted souvenirs. Pack out everything.

Camping

Canaveral National Seashore

The seashore's fourteen primitive campsites are not located on the Florida peninsula but on designated natural sand and spoil islands in the Intracoastal Waterway and Mosquito Lagoon. The islands can be reached only by powerboat, canoe, or kayak.

Campsites are $20 a night and can be reserved up to six months in advance. Sites 1–5 are reserved for campers who rent a canoe from the National Seashore. Canoes hold a maximum of two people plus their gear. Bring several gallon water jugs; the islands have no fresh water.

For canoe rental information, contact the Apollo Beach Visitor Center or call (386) 428-3384, ext. 0. To rent a campsite, visit recreation.gov and go to "Camping & Lodging" or call (877) 444-6777. At times, fishing in the Indian River is very good. A saltwater license is required.

Florida State Parks

About 57 of Florida's 190 state parks offer camping, providing more than 7,500 camping, cabin, and RV sites. Reservations can be made up to eleven months in advance by calling (800) 326-3521 between 8 a.m. and 8 p.m. or visiting reserve .floridastateparks.org/Web/.

Although the parks stay open until sunset year-round, check-in is between 8 a.m. and 5 p.m. Fees range from $5 to $60 according to park location, season, and whether a site has water and electricity. Cabins range from $30 to $180.

Not all state parks allow pets in campgrounds. For parks that do allow pets, check floridastateparks.org/PetPolicy under "Pet Camping."

If you plan to spend considerable time in Central Florida's state parks, consider purchasing the annual entrance passes for individuals and for families of up to eight people. They are available online at floridastateparks.org/learn/florida-state-parks -annual-pass-discount, at a park, through the mail, or by calling (352) 628-7002. The cost is $60 for an individual, $120 for a family. Discounted Military Annual passes also are available. Free lifetime Military Entrance passes are provided for disabled vets and their surviving spouses. Camping fees are rarely covered.

Anyone traveling around the state by RV should enjoy the park facilities. Tent campers, on the other hand, may find the close-together spaces at some parks a little claustrophobic. Fortunately, some state parks and national and state forests offer camping at primitive sites deep in the woods.

Primitive sites require backpacking everything in. A site may offer a chemical toilet, a fire ring, and possibly a picnic table. It's wiser to count on only a clear space.

For questions about Florida State Parks, including entrance fee schedules, call (850) 245-2157 or visit floridastateparks.org.

Florida State Forests

State forests have developed campgrounds in certain locations with electrical and water hookups, fire rings, picnic tables, and centralized restrooms with showers. The campsite fee is $15 per night and sites are reserved at floridastateforests.reserve america.com.

Primitive campsites and group camps have limited amenities that vary by location. All provide a backcountry experience in a remote setting for a fee of $10 per person per night. To reserve, contact the specific state forest office for a permit. Links to all the state forests are found at fdacs.gov/Forest-Wildfire/Our-Forests/State-Forests.

The earliest campsite check-in time is usually 3 p.m. The latest checkout time is 1 p.m., unless otherwise posted. Chain saws cannot be used at campsites; collect fallen dead wood for campfires. Campfires are permitted only in designated locations.

Whenever a particular Florida county is placed under a tropical storm or hurricane warning by the National Weather Service, state forest campsites and recreation areas located in that county close immediately.

Florida Wildlife Management Areas

To camp in a wildlife management area (WMA), make a reservation two weeks in advance and obtain a free permit from the FWC. It's possible to apply for a maximum of fourteen consecutive days within a month. Fees, other requirements, and regulations vary by location. Campsites tend to be primitive and may be seasonal. Advance permission may also be necessary simply to enter a WMA. Contact details for each WMA is available at https://myfwc.com/recreation/camping/.

Ocala National Forest

Ocala National Forest offers both developed and primitive campgrounds. Developed sites without electricity start at $20. RV sites with power average $65. Day-use fees must be paid in advance online at recreation.gov or at the entrance with the recreation.gov mobile app.

Whether camping at a recreation area or at a primitive site, take special care with a campfire, which may be prohibited in dry conditions. You are responsible for keeping your fire under control. Never leave a fire unattended, and always make certain it is completely out before leaving camp.

Ocala also allows no-cost dispersed primitive camping in selected areas along the Florida Trail. Camping is not permitted near developed recreation areas or within 150 yards of another campsite, building, recreation area, or occupied area. The monthly stay limit is fourteen days, and the campsite maximum is five people. Quiet hours are 10 p.m. to 6 a.m.

Dispersed camping is allowed only in designated sites or in places specifically provided and marked for dispersed camping. These locations include the Alexander Springs Wilderness, Billie Bay Wilderness, Davenport Landing and Davenport Landing Trail, Juniper Prairie Wilderness, Little Lake George Wilderness, and the St. Francis Trailhead. For more information visit fs.usda.gov/activity/florida/recreation/camping-cabins/?recid=70792&actid=34.

It is mandatory that campers use a bear-proof canister to prevent bears from smelling or having access to your food supplies. For complete details see fs.usda.gov/detail/florida/home/?cid=FSBDEV3_008653.

The Trail

Many blazes on Florida trails have been placed there by the Florida Trail Association (FTA). The eye-level blazes are normally quite easy to spot. This is the FTA trail marking system:

- Orange blazes mark the main trail.
- Blue blazes designate side trails to developed campgrounds or a natural site of unusual interest. (In some Florida state forests, blue blazes also mark an equestrian trail.)
- White blazes mark the hiking trails in many state parks and preserves.
- A double blaze signals a change in direction. It could also mean the trail is no longer taking the most obvious route. Don't leave a double blaze until you've spotted the next single blaze.
- Use a map in sections where the Florida Trail is not blazed.

Dog-friendly

Your dog is not welcome on many hiking trails. One reason is that small dogs are a favorite alligator snack. For public health reasons, dogs are also not welcome near most swimming areas, including beaches, playgrounds, bathing areas and cabins, park buildings, and concession facilities. When dogs are allowed in a park or recreation area, they must be kept on a 6-foot leash and confined to a picnic or camping area. To be honest, in many instances it's much less hassle for both you and your dog if your pet stays at home.

Safety

Wild animals shouldn't be a major concern as long you use a bear-proof canister and/or a bear-proof bag when wilderness camping. Getting lost shouldn't be much of a problem either; trails are well marked, and a cell phone should work on most hikes in

Dog owners are reminded that bringing their pet on a hiking trail is a privilege that could be revoked because some owners used the trail as a poop dumping ground.

this guide. Check your mobile company's coverage map to be certain. Service can be spotty in thick forest, deep in a swamp, or in an unusually remote area. Realistically, only the larger mobile service providers should be relied on for navigating a hike by phone.

Carry a hiking stick on trails known for rough conditions.

To avoid polluting with plastic, consider carrying two sealed mason jars in a fanny pack. Or use insulated water bottles filled with water and some ice. Cold or cool water on a hike makes a big difference.

Always carry insect repellent—you may need to apply it more than once. And don't forget the sunblock.

The following safety topics are intended to provide a safe and enjoyable hiking experience.

Weather

Flat, easy terrain is the big plus of Central Florida hiking. Regrettably, there are seasonal factors that make walking much less enjoyable. Keep in mind that Florida weather forecasts are often inaccurate because conditions can change so quickly.

Although it is warm between May and October, hypothermia is sometimes a possibility in cooler months. This dangerous condition usually occurs in the 30- to

50-degree air temperature range. Hypothermia typically happens when it rains unexpectedly and a wet hiker is exposed to a cold and chilly wind. Hypothermia occurs when the body loses heat faster than it is able to produce it. Carry a light windbreaker or space blanket to help avoid hypothermia.

Lightning

Frequent thunderstorm activity makes Florida one of the world's lightning capitals. On average, forty-nine people die annually in the United States due to lightning, seven of them in Florida. Most deaths occur in coastal areas, especially beaches.

In Central Florida you're more likely to be zapped by lightning than fatally bitten by a rattlesnake (which also are at their liveliest in summer). Thunderstorms start in mid-May. July and August usually are the peak lightning months, but June and September also may have frequent thunderstorms. Sometimes it seems lightning accompanies every summer rain.

You will be safer when a thunderstorm approaches by doing the following:

- Stay away from the beach or any type of water.
- Try to get through the storm in a low spot under a thick stand of small trees, but don't stand on the roots.
- Avoid tall trees in open fields, trees at the water's edge, or trees whose roots are in damp soil.
- Don't shelter under oaks or pine trees. Their high starch content makes them good natural conductors of electricity.
- If you're wearing an aluminum-frame backpack, take it off—and stay well away from it until the storm passes.
- Stay away from wire fences or any metal that could conduct lightning to you.
- A tingling sensation in your scalp is a warning that a bolt may be about to strike: Fall to the ground immediately.

Hurricanes

Named for Huracan, the Mayan god of wind, storm, and fire, hurricanes may severely impact hiking conditions. Hurricane season begins in June, with the greatest activity typically in August, September, and October. As the saying about Florida's hurricane season goes: "June too soon, July stand by, August and September remember, October all over." The jingle needs updating; hurricanes have been appearing in October and November as well.

Hurricanes can have devastating impacts on hiking trails. Severe storms and accompanying tornadoes may uproot thousands of trees and seriously damage trails. Some trails may have to be rerouted temporarily; others may close until footbridges are replaced. After a storm, always check the websites for where you want to hike. See what damage, if any, was caused. Repairs can take many months. The Florida Trail

This tree was snapped like a twig some time ago. The impact from tropical storms can be visible for years afterward.

Association keeps a record of which parts to the Florida Trail are closed at floridatrail.org/trail-closures-and-notices.

Heat and Humidity

The biggest drawbacks to Central Florida hiking, heat and humidity-- also pose the greatest dangers for hikers. Summer days simply become too hot to hike comfortably except during early morning. This is why most of the Florida Trail is not maintained between May and October, when comparatively few people hike.

The Sun

The closer to the equator, the higher the UV radiation level. At Florida's low latitude, you receive more UV radiation than almost anywhere else in the continental United States. Because the Florida sun is so intense, gradual exposure helps avoid painful sunburn unless you already have a base tan. Visitors are advised to spend only 20 to 30 minutes in direct sun on their first day. The sun is at its worst between 10 a.m. and 3 p.m.

Water-resistant broad-spectrum sunscreen or sunblock is shown to be effective at reducing the risk of skin cancer. A sun protection factor (SPF) of 25 or 50 is much more effective than an SPF of 15. Cover all exposed body parts, including the back of your ears. Also apply sunscreen/block to your jaw and the lower part of your neck, plus the upper chest area exposed to sun. Some people may need to wear sunblock on their lips.

Cover up with a long-sleeved shirt and long pants, and wear a broad-brimmed hat. Lightweight clothing labeled "UPF" (ultraviolet protection factor) offers varied levels of shielding just like sunscreens. Regrettably, the shirts and pants often are made of materials unsuited to Florida's hot humid weather, and an outfit turns into a sauna suit. Cotton is the most breathable fabric, but it provides less sun protection than synthetic materials.

Sunglasses are needed for most Central Florida hiking. They are a necessity around lakes and coastal areas. Constant exposure to bright sunlight can cause headaches and fatigue. Use polarized sunglasses that block out harmful ultraviolet rays and reduce glare.

Clouds may create a false sense of security when they hide the sun. The sun may be hidden, but it still can inflict a severe burn. Beach hikers receive a double whammy: from the sun overhead and the rays reflected off the water and sand. In the event of sunburn, apply aloe gel. It is not only soothing but also often prevents blistering and peeling.

Heatstroke

Heatstroke, also called sunstroke, is caused by staying out in the sun too long, causing the body temperature to rise to 104°F or higher. This is a life-threatening medical emergency requiring immediate treatment. Symptoms of oncoming sunstroke are dizziness, vertigo, fevers, blistering, headache, nausea, sudden lack of sweat, and delusions. If these symptoms occur, take a cool bath or shower and stay in an air-conditioned area. Use replenishing drink mixes to replace lost body fluids. If you don't feel better, contact a doctor.

Heat Exhaustion

Heat exhaustion is less serious but still of major concern. Symptoms are headache, nausea, dizziness, weakness, unsteady gait, muscle cramps, and fatigue. The best treatment is to drink water or replenishing drink mixes, soak with towels, take a cool bath, and stay in air-conditioning.

Prickly Heat

The constant humidity may cause a rash. Help avoid rashes by applying powder with zinc in the morning and evening. Also wear loose-fitting pants. The most comfortable shirts for hiking are usually made of lightweight cotton.

Water

You sweat a lot in high humidity, and not replacing that liquid will make you feel tired and cranky. Dehydration is the greatest danger faced by hikers in Central Florida. Thirst, dry lips, and a parched throat all are signs of dehydration. It takes about two weeks for someone on vacation to adjust to the state's high humidity.

As a general rule, *no water source* along Florida trails is safe to drink unless it is clearly designated as potable. Don't let clear spring water fool you: What you can't see could harm you. If spring or river water needs to be used for cooking, boil it for about 5 minutes to kill parasites. Or use a water filter designed to remove biological pathogens, including giardia. Drinking directly from a spring can cause gastroenteritis, diarrhea, and vomiting.

Always plan to carry your own liquid on hikes. Keep your hands free by using a fanny pack/belt bag/waist pack with two water bottle holders. Or, if temperature allows, put water bottles in the pockets of a hiking vest or lightweight mesh backpack's side pocket.

Consume liquids even when you're not thirsty. If you wait until you are thirsty, you could already be dehydrated. Some experts suggest drinking 16 ounces of liquids a couple of hours before you start out, then scheduling drink stops every half hour whether you feel you need them or not. You may drink a gallon of liquid on a long day's hike, so plan accordingly. Consider using one of the replenishing liquids sold to restore important electrolytes lost by sweating. Juice and other sweet drinks take longer to be absorbed by the body.

Someone who develops cramps after drinking a lot of water may be low on potassium. It is easily replenished by taking a potassium supplement, eating a banana, or eating something with ketchup on it.

The common golden silk spider is a harmless orb weaver that sometimes builds its web across a narrow section of trail. If you tear it down, the spider often builds a new one by the next day.

Insects and Arachnids

Central Florida's subtropical climate has blessed it with an awful lot of creepy-crawlies. But with proper precautions, you can avoid them all. Literally hundreds of thousands of Floridians hike every season without ever getting an insect bite.

Knowing what to expect is like taking a course in defensive driving. You'll rarely need to call on the knowledge. Consider the following critters merely subjects of interest, not inevitable irritants.

Mosquitoes

You may be interested (or disturbed) to learn that Florida has eighty species of mosquitoes. It also is the nation's mosquito capital. Saltwater mosquitoes are active year-round in coastal areas because of their access to water for breeding.

Freshwater mosquitoes are most active in the rainy season. After heavy rains, you may encounter mosquitoes wherever you hike. Fortunately, mosquitoes tend to be scarce until twilight. When that time approaches, get off the trail, stand near a smoky fire, or hide in a tent.

Mosquito bites usually are only annoying. Occasionally there are outbreaks of encephalitis and West Nile virus. The National Centers for Disease Control and Protection (CDC) advises that your best protection is insect repellent containing DEET. You can also spray clothing with repellents containing permethrin or another EPA-registered repellent so that mosquitoes won't bite through thin clothing. Never apply repellents containing permethrin directly to exposed skin. For the latest CDC tips, visit cdc.gov/westnile/index.html.

Chiggers

These small red mites are fond of attacking the ankles, waist area, and wrists, where they burrow under the skin and cause itching. Applying clear nail polish to chigger bites will often smother any critters still in the skin. Calamine lotion helps relieve the itching. The best way to avoid the pesky critters is to spray DEET on your socks, pants legs, and waist area. This seems to repel chiggers better than anything else.

Fire Ants

Fire ant mounds are readily spotted—they look like shovelfuls of dirt or white sand. The danger is accidentally stepping on a small mound and having the ants swarm up your legs. As many as half a million fire ants live in a colony. Anyone allergic to ant bites should carry appropriate medication with them. If you're bitten, the allergy medication Benadryl helps stop the itching. Applying hydrocortisone cream to the bites helps reduce itchiness or a rash.

Ticks

Because of Central Florida's warm weather, ticks are active almost year-round. Due to the danger of Lyme disease, it is essential to always use repellent in the woods. Check your clothing and body for ticks after a hike. When camping, spray your tent and sleeping bag with repellent. The CDC suggests taking a single prophylactic dose of Doxycycline (200 mg for an adult) to reduce the risk of Lyme disease after a tick bite.

No-see-ums

For the most part, only beach hikers at sunrise and sunset need to worry about no-see-ums. These midges or sand flies are so tiny to be almost invisible. Long pants and shoes and socks are the best protection.

Scorpions

Found most often in the dry regions of Central Florida, scorpions are known to crawl into hiking boots at night. So shake out your boots before putting them on, or keep them wrapped in a plastic bag in your tent. Scorpion stings are painful but rarely fatal.

Spiders

Only two species of spiders in Central Florida are considered a serious threat to humans: the black widow and the brown recluse.

Black widow spiders live in woodpiles, inside stone and wood walls, in outdoor toilets—anywhere that offers a good hiding place. A black widow bite may cause redness, pain, and swelling around the wound. It can also progress to abdominal cramping, nausea, and sweating. The only remedy is a visit to the hospital for antivenin.

The only other spider to be concerned about is the brown recluse, also known as the fiddleback or violin spider because of the distinctive violin-shaped marking on its back. The brown recluse is not deadly, but the venom from its bite actually causes body tissue around the inflicted area to disintegrate. Without medical treatment, the wound will continue to deepen and can take months to heal.

Poisonous Plants and Fungi

There are about fifty species of poisonous plants and fungi in Florida. These include oleander and several types of mushrooms, but most are troublesome only if you ingest them. It's best not to dine on anything you find growing in the wild.

Touching poison ivy or poison sumac may produce kin irritation, including small, itchy blisters. Poison ivy is recognizable as a shrub or vine with three leaflets on each leaf and whitish berries. Poison sumac is a bush with seven to thirteen leaflets and white berries. Cortisone cream is an effective remedy for both. So is water hot enough to hurt but not burn you. Watch where you walk and where you sit, and these plants should not be a problem.

Animals

Snakes

Florida has a larger snake population than any other southeastern state, yet snakes are rarely a problem if you stick to the trails, don't haphazardly step over logs without looking, and exercise common sense.

Six Florida snakes are venomous. Half of them are rattlesnakes: the eastern diamondback, timber/canebrake, and pygmy rattlesnake. Florida's other venomous snakes are the cottonmouth water moccasin, coral snake, and copperhead (found mostly in the Panhandle). The cottonmouth, found in swampy areas, is the most aggressive. It has been known to charge at people who unknowingly block the snake's access to a favorite place.

The multicolored coral snake is related to mambas and cobras. Said to be the nation's most venomous snake, it is rarely a concern. It's less aggressive and must almost gnaw on you to break your skin. Most bites occur when people pick up "the pretty snake" to examine it. Coral snakes make their homes in brush piles, rotting logs, and pinewoods.

The coral snake sometimes is confused with the harmless king snake, which also has colorful bands. The way to tell the two apart: "Red touch yellow, kill a fellow; red touch black, won't hurt Jack." Not great poetry, but it makes its point.

If someone is bitten by any kind of venomous snake, the best treatment usually is to do nothing except take the person immediately to a hospital. Cutting the skin and attempting to suck out the venom often does considerable harm, sometimes severing muscle tissue.

Black Bears and Raccoons

When camping overnight in Central Florida, take steps not to be raided by either a black bear or a pack of raccoons. They all want to steal the food you've brought into their territory. Black bears supposedly can smell food from two miles away. They also probably know exactly what food is sealed in a plastic bag stored in a cooler in a locked car trunk. You need to lock them out.

Keep food hidden and protected inside a vehicle when possible. Never leave anything tasty on a picnic table or leave a cooler unattended. Brightly colored potato chips bags are not an unfamiliar sight to black bears or raccoons. Keep these and other snacks out of sight. Store only water jugs in your tent, never food.

When hiking in Ocala National Forest, it is mandatory to use a bear-proof canister for food and "attractants." Black bear and camper interactions have occasionally been so serious that parts of the national forest have been closed due to overly aggressive bears.

Raccoons can be another campsite pest. They've had decades to associate food with humans because trash cans at numerous campgrounds were left without tops or the lids were too easy to remove. Like children, raccoons are attracted to shiny objects, so hide those. To deter the animals after dark, spray the area with vinegar or place rags soaked in ammonia around your campsite.

Rabies in raccoons can be a concern, although the CDC reports that only one person has ever died from a rabid raccoon bite. An infected animal is likely to be either overly friendly or aggressive. A staggering gait, discharge from the eyes or mouth, wet and matted hair on the face, and repeated high-pitched vocalizations are

Bear-proof food bags and canisters are required in some areas due to increased bear activity around hikers and campers.

other signs of rabies. If anyone is bitten, they must receive a rabies vaccine shot within 72 hours for it to be effective. There is no cure for rabies once the symptoms appear, and it is virtually 100 percent fatal.

Alligators

This reptile is far down the list of problem animals for a reason. Unless you swim in a remote lake during the spring mating season (when alligators sometimes may go a little crazy) or during low water levels, when they have been known to attack swimmers and even a lakeside jogger, gators should not pose a danger. Alligators normally run or disappear when they encounter a human. However, their behavior will be different if people have been feeding them or if you are accompanied by a small dog (a favorite alligator snack).

Never harass an alligator or get between the animal and its body of water and all should be fine. Alligators usually are aggressive only when provoked, protecting their nest, or during spring mating season. It is extremely rare for an alligator to chase people.

If You Get Lost

Frankly, this will take some doing on the trails in this book. But it can happen when someone chases after a dog that should have been leashed or a child suddenly runs off to go exploring. Better to stay where you are and try calling the escapee back to you.

If that doesn't work, don't chase blindly. You need to keep your sense of direction in order to retrace your steps. Remain aware of the direction you came from and you should be able to return to your trail.

Always carry a map and a compass. Take a flashlight in case you don't make it back before dark. Or download a compass and flashlight app to your phone. Before hiking, link to the trail you're hiking. A Google or Apple map also might provide the assistance you need. If you are really desperate, phone someone at the trailhead for assistance if possible. Some trails have location or GPS markers that should help guide your rescuers.

For backup, carry a whistle. Three whistle blasts is a universal distress signal. To make a proper distress signal, make each blast last for about 3 seconds, which you can count off in your head. Pause for several minutes, then start again. The noise should guide people to you if they have to come searching.

Hunting

If this were a perfect world, all hiking problems would vanish with cool weather. But just as the weather turns cooler, usually around mid-November, gun hunting season begins. That is of concern to hikers because parts of the Florida National Scenic Trail pass through national forests and wildlife management areas open to hunting.

Hiking is forbidden in many areas during the first week of the hunting season and also the period between Christmas and New Year's, when hunting is at its peak. During hunting season, hikers must wear a fluorescent orange vest (available at sporting goods stores). Never wear anything white—white-tailed deer is the favorite target.

Trails located in hunting areas are clearly identified in a hike's description. Hunting season dates are available from the Florida Fish and Wildlife Conservation Commission: myfwc.com/hunting/season-dates.

In some regions, archery season begins as early as August. It is quickly followed by crossbow and muzzle-loading gun seasons. The majority of hikes in this book are not in hunting areas.

Hiking with Children

In planning any outing with children, remember with whom you are hiking. Don't be surprised or upset when they act like kids. Children as young as 5 or 6 are often capable of hiking for short distances, but not all-day hikes. It's amazing how a youngster who seems an endless bundle of energy at home can tire so quickly outdoors, especially if it's too warm or the hike is not interesting enough.

Short nature walks like those at the front of this guide will have more appeal than a 2-hour jaunt through the woods where the scenery doesn't change much. Boardwalks into swamps usually lead to interesting places full of birdlife or unusual trees, such as a virgin stand of giant cypress trees wearing long swaying beards of grayish-white Spanish moss. Interesting nature walks and interpretive trails are the easiest way to create a lifelong interest in the outdoors and all its diversity.

Pack snacks to maintain everyone's energy on the trail. Dried fruit, candy, and granola bars all supply good fuel. When you graduate to overnight trips, freeze-dried dinners are easy and convenient. Some can even be prepared in the pouch simply by adding boiling water—but only if you haven't raised picky eaters.

Young skin is sensitive to the sun, so always apply sunblock to your kids before and during your hike. A good bug repellant, preferably not too strong, should be a standard part of your kit. Have bug bite relief ready and antihistamines to reduce swelling and itching, such as Benadryl Itch Stopping Gel, an over-the-counter anti-itch cream.

A hat helps keep the sun out of sensitive young eyes. Rain gear is another important consideration, since kids often have less tolerance for cold than adults. If your camp will be near open water, consider bringing a life vest for your child.

To sustain your child's interest between outings, take them shopping and allow them to choose their own walking shoes, fanny packs, day sacks, water bottles, whatever. You may need to offer some guidance here and there, but let them feel that they are making all the important decisions.

Children learn from their parents by example. Hiking and camping trips are excellent opportunities to teach young ones to tread lightly and minimize their imprint upon the environment.

This warning about possibly dangerous wild animals in an area is to inform you—and also to help absolve the property owner of any liability.

Trail Descriptions

Almost all of the forty Central Florida trails described here are true hiking experiences on trails not shared with cyclists, skateboarders, or horses. With the popularity of mountain biking, it's getting harder to find pure hiking trails. The guide's few multiuse trails are clearly labeled as such.

Hiking Central Florida does not attempt to cover every trail in Central Florida, only some of the best and most varied ones. All offer the chance to visit natural places that show Florida at its finest. Included are several nature and historical preserves with hiking trails that offer the chance to explore truly unique or historic sites.

The walks in this guide are divided into four categories: **Short Family Hikes** ranging from 1 to 3 miles; **Day Hikes**, from 3 to 12 miles; **Overnight Hikes** with easy access to primitive campsites; and **Long Haulers**, true backpacking experiences that require a weekend or more to complete.

The map at the beginning of this book pinpoints where the trails are. The descriptions contain the information you need to be well prepared for your hiking adventure. Each hike starts by covering the following topics:

Start: Identifies where the hike starts.

Distance: This lets you know how far it is from the parking lot or trailhead to the end of the path and back again.

Difficulty: Each trail is evaluated according to difficulty, which is usually based on its length since the terrain normally is flat. These estimates do not take into account wet or muddy conditions resulting from prolonged rains or other natural events.

Hiking time: The times given for all hikes are not based on how fast you could walk a trail but what is reasonable for someone on a casual stroll who wants to look around and stop and take pictures.

Seasons: What is the best time of year to hike in Florida? Almost always from November to early May. Heat, humidity, and frequent rains take the joy out of summer hikes.

Fees and permits: Almost every hiking area has implemented user fees in recent years. They range from $2 per person to $20 per vehicle. If you intend to visit an area frequently, inquire about the cost of an annual pass. Florida state forests require that day-use permits be purchased online in advance. Other agencies are likely to require this.

Trail contact: This category lists the name of the managing agency, its address, and its website and phone number. Always check the website a day for two before your planned hike to avoid surprises.

Many public areas require day-use fees to be paid online.

Schedule: Most hikes are on public and private lands with set opening and closing times. This section has the times when the hiking trails are open.

Dog-friendly: Dogs are not welcome on all hiking trails. One reason is that alligators like to eat dogs. For health reasons, dogs are also not permitted around most swimming areas, including beaches, playgrounds, and bathing areas. This section tells you whether pets are permitted on that particular hike. Service dogs are welcome in state and national parks.

Trail surface: The material that makes up the trail.

Land status: Which agency manages the land on which the trail lies.

Nearest town: The city or town with minimal visitor services closest to the trailhead.

Other trail users: Those most likely to share the trail with you.

Water availability: Plan on bringing your own. If water is available for a hike, it likely will be near the trailhead, at a visitor center or restroom, but this is not something you should count on.

Maps: The maps are based on topographic maps issued by the State of Florida and those supplied by the USDA Forest Service and the Florida State Parks. We used the *DeLorme: Florida Atlas & Gazetteer* as an additional resource.

Special considerations: This is not included with every hike. It most often deals with hunting and the need to wear fluorescent orange. It could also feature especially good accessible facilities.

Each summer the annual hunting calendar is published online at myfwc.com/hunting/season-dates.

Amenities: This section lists services such as campsites restrooms, picnic tables, shelter, and which accessible facilities are present.

Cell service: This answers the question about whether there is cell service in the parking lot or along the trail.

Trail conditions: A description of the trail surface and other considerations.

Overnight lodging/camping: These categories appear only with those hikes that offer these options.

Finding the trailhead: Detailed driving directions are provided to each hike's location and to where you should park. A current Florida map or GPS directions should guide you to your starting point. With the exception of Florida wildlife management areas and some Florida state forests, most roads to trailheads are paved. A family car can handle these routes easily.

Trailhead GPS: Decimal degrees, noting latitude and longitude geographic coordinates as decimal fractions of a degree, such as 28.9368 / -80.8302. This is not the coordinate system Google Earth uses, but it does recognize it.

The Hike: The hike description.

Miles and directions: A detailed route finder with distances between trail landmarks so you know what to look for on your hike.

More information: Other hikes and points of interest in the area.

Trail Finder

Hike Number	Hike Locations	Fishing	Cabins	Primitive Camping	Campground	Swimming	Canoeing/ Kayaking	Bicycling	Beach	Wildlife Viewing
1	Bulow Plantation Ruins Historic State Park	X					X	X		X
2–5	Canaveral National Seashore	X		X		X	X	X	X	X
6–7	Honeymoon Island State Park	X				X	X	X	X	X
8	Caladesi Island State Park	X				X	X		X	X
9–10	Lake Woodruff National Wildlife Refuge	X						X		X
11	Hontoon Island State Park	X	X	X			X	X		X
12	Blue Spring State Park		X	X	X	X	X	X		X
13	Geneva Wilderness Area	X		X				X		X
14	Tibet-Butler Preserve									X
15	Withlacoochee State Forest	X		X	X	X	X	X		X
16–17	Bulow Plantation Ruins Historic State Park and Bulow Creek State Park							X		X
18–20	Merritt Island National Wildlife Refuge	X					X	X		X
21	De Leon Springs State Park					X	X			X
22	Black Bear Wilderness Area	X		X						X
23	Little Big Econ State Forest	X		X		~		X		X
24	Split Oak Forest Wildlife and Environmental Area									X
25–26	The Nature Conservancy's Disney Wilderness Preserve									X
27–28	Hillsborough River State Park			X	X		X	X		X
29–30	Tiger Creek Preserve									X
31–32	Prairie Lakes Unit—Three Lakes Wildlife Management Area	X						X		X
33	Little Manatee River State Park			X			X	X		X
34–35	Seminole State Forest	X		X				X		X
36	Wekiwa Springs State Park			X	X	X	X	X	X	X
37–38	Lake Kissimmee State Park	X		X	X		X	X		X
39	Ocala National Forest—Ocala North			X	X	X	X	X		X
40	Ocala National Forest—Ocala South	X		X	X	X	X	X		X

Map Legend

Transportation

Interstate Highway	═══〔4〕═══
US Highway	══〔27〕══
State Highway	══〔19〕══
County Road	═〔CR 525〕═
Dirt Road	═ ══ ══ ═
Railroad	├──┼──┼──┤
Featured Trail	■■■■■■■■
Other Trail	- - - - - - -

Hydrology

Lake/Reservoir	
River/Creek	
Marsh/Swamp	☆ ☆
Mangrove Swamps	
Rapids	∥

Land Use

Wildlife Preserve	
State Park/State Forest	

Symbols

Boat Ramp	⛴
Bridge	⋈
Campground	▲
Cemetery	⚰
Chapel	⛪
City/Town	○
Gate	⚲
Interpretive Trail	🚶
Marina	⚓
Parking	🅿
Picnic Area	⛺
Point of Interest	■
Ranger Station	👤
Restroom	🚻
Tower	♜
Trailhead (Start)	❶
Viewpoint	✷
Visitor Information	❓

Short Family Hikes

Bulow Plantation Ruins Historic State Park

Entry road to the Bulow Plantation ruins

A short but striking section of the Florida National Scenic Trail (FNST) starts from the ruins of the largest sugar mill on Florida's east coast, destroyed in 1836 during the Second Seminole War. Altogether, there were three Seminole Wars in Florida. The Seminoles were never defeated and never signed a peace treaty with the US government. No other Indian tribe can make that claim.

Remains of the plantation include extensive ruins of the sugar mill, a spring-house, and the crumbling foundation of the great house. The buildings were made of coquina (co-KEEN-a), a sedimentary rock found along the Florida coast.

At the sugar mill, interpretive signs explain the process for making syrup from sugarcane. An adjacent small building contains artifacts found on the grounds. A loop walk with a short spur trail leads to the spring house. The featured hike begins on the plantation's one-of-a-kind entry road.

Start: Parking lot near park entrance
Distance: 1.5 miles
Difficulty: Easy
Hiking time: About 1 hour
Seasons: Nov–May
Fees and permits: Park admission $4 per vehicle

Trail contact: Bulow Plantation Ruins Historic State Park, 3501 Old Kings Rd., Flagler Beach 32136; (386) 517-2084; floridastateparks.org/parks-and-trails/bulow-plantation-ruins-historic-state-park
Schedule: 9 a.m. to 5 p.m. Mon and Thurs through Sun; closed Tues and Wed

Dog-friendly: Leashed dogs permitted
Trail surface: Dirt path, some paved areas
Land status: Florida state park
Nearest town: Flagler Beach
Other trail users: Cyclists
Water availability: None; bring your own. Nearby Tomoka State Park has more complete facilities.
Maps: Available at nearby Tomoka State Park (386-676-4050), 4.5 miles south of Bulow Creek State Park on Old Dixie Highway. None really needed.

Special considerations: Accessible restrooms and a picnic pavilion. Service animals are welcome.
Amenities: Nature trails, bicycling, and picnicking. More activities are available at adjacent Tomoka State Park, not Bulow Ruins.
Cell service: Good
Trail conditions: The ruins area is normally dry with flat ground in most places. The Nature Trail may be wet after rain. Have bug repellent handy.

1 Bulow Plantation Ruins Trail

Distance: 1.5-mile loop

Finding the trailhead: Take exit 268 off I-95 and travel east less than a mile on Old Dixie Highway to CR 2001 (Old Kings Road), on the left. Go north 2 miles to the brown-and-white state marker at Plantation Road, called Monument Road on some maps. Turn right into Bulow Plantation Ruins Historic State Park. Parking for the hike is in the parking area just before the park gate. Have the correct entrance fee for the envelope fed into the Iron Ranger. Tear off and display the stub on your dash. Trailhead GPS: 29.434253 / -81.138069

The Hike

Slowly drive down the Bulow Plantation Road through a long and impressive archway of stately old forest. One of Florida's most impressive entrances to anywhere, it continues for almost a full mile. The thick woodland canopy perfectly curves over the dirt road and blocks the view and noise of the developments that surround the park up to its borders.

This perfectly formed entry road, a time tunnel blocking out the modern day, allows you to enjoy the quiet and peaceful setting in one of Florida's most timeless state parks.

This hike lets you appreciate at least a small portion of the entry road's scenery. Park at the trailhead just outside the park's official entrance gate. The small parking area (fee) is for longer and more difficult Bulow Woods hikes 16 and 17. The ruins walk is an easy one unless there are pockets of deep sand between the parking lot and the Nature Trail, just 0.2 mile away.

Lock your vehicle and begin your hike into the plantation ruins park. Those parked outside the entrance gate do not need to pay the admission fee, but you can by placing the exact amount in an envelope and tearing off a strip as your proof of purchase.

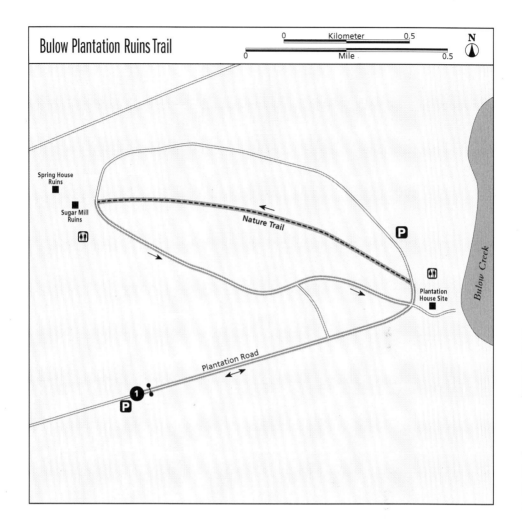

Hike slowly though the dwindling corridor of trees on the narrow road. A road on the left will be your return walk after touring the Sugar Mill Ruins. The entry road curves left and arrives at the Nature Trail to the Sugar Mill Ruins and Slave Quarters Site, also located on the left. Directly opposite the trailhead is a picnic pavilion and, possibly, an open restroom. If those facilities aren't open, they're available at the ruins site.

The Nature Trail leads through a fairly open hammock of oaks and saw palmetto. The walk familiarizes you with the natural conditions during the plantation days, but there is no indication whether any of the clearings beside the trail were slave quarters.

The trail exit is across from the Bulow Plantation Sugar Mill Ruins. The buildings, made of thousands of small coquina shells, still exhibit scorch marks from when Seminoles attacked the site almost 200 years ago. Still standing tall is part of the huge thick-walled sugar mill, where sugarcane was crushed and boiled.

Ruins of the Bulow Plantation

Interpretive signs placed around the damaged buildings create an informative self-guided tour. Visitors must remain on the paved paths to avoid accidentally damaging anything at the site.

On the left and next to the site is a covered area with several large information panels that further tell the plantation's history and artifacts from the era. There are also restrooms here.

Now a burned-out shell, the once-magnificent Bulow Plantation was built in 1821 by Charles Bulow of Charleston, South Carolina. Using slave labor, he cleared much of the 2,500 acres for sugarcane, cotton, rice, and indigo. Bulow died after only three years of working the estate.

The property was taken over by his son, John, who fashioned it into one of the finest and wealthiest plantations in Florida. This sugar mill was one of the largest ever built in the state and the largest along Florida's east coast. It became known as Bulow Ville. Bulow Plantation was destroyed by the Seminole Indians because the federal government had implemented a program to move the Seminole Indians to reservations in the far west. Bulow opposed the plan, but the Seminoles didn't care about his support. He occupied what they considered to be their land. Realizing the Seminoles were increasingly hostile, Bulow and his slaves abandoned the plantation.

Refusing to submit to the territorial government's policy of forcible removal, Seminoles attacked and destroyed sixteen plantations along the St. Johns and Halifax Rivers in 1835. In January 1836, the Seminoles attacked and burned every plantation built on land the Indians claimed belonged to them. This included Bulow's plantation. Disheartened, Bulow gave up and moved away. It's said he died before the age of 27.

To return to the trailhead, go right on the dirt road in front of the ruins. Stay on the road until you return to the road you hiked in on. Turn right to return to the trailhead.

Miles and Directions

0.0 Start at the north trailhead parking lot for the Bulow Woods Linear and Loop Hikes.

0.2 Arrive at the trailhead for the nature walk leading to the ruins.

0.33 The Nature Trail ends across the street from the Bulow Plantation Sugar Mills Ruins. Follow the signs around the ruins.

1.5 Arrive back at the Bulow Woods trailhead and parking lot.

Canaveral National Seashore

The distance from the Florida–Georgia border to Key West is more than 500 miles. For all that distance, the longest stretch of undeveloped beach remaining on Florida's east coast is the 25-mile strip of barrier island known as Canaveral National Seashore.

When the Kennedy Space Center was developed on Merritt Island in the early 1960s, NASA found it had far more land than it needed. So NASA invited two other government agencies to help manage the area. The US Fish and Wildlife Service established the Merritt Island National Wildlife Refuge as a sanctuary for wintering waterfowl in 1963. In 1975 the National Park Service created Canaveral National Seashore. The national seashore's close connection to the space program is still obvious: Its southernmost boundary is in plain view of one of the old space shuttle launchpads.

Start: Canaveral National Seashore is composed of three beaches: Apollo, Klondike, and Playalinda. Its four short nature walks are located at Apollo Beach at the northern end of the national seashore.

Elevation gain: Virtually none except a boardwalk reaching 50 feet high

Distance: Four hikes totaling under 5 miles

Difficulty: Easy

Hiking time: Four short hikes in different locations take 20–30 minutes each. All Canaveral National Seashore Nature Trails are located in the Apollo Beach section along the Indian River. The hikes are described from north to south.

Seasons: Nov to May for the most hospitable weather. Beware of mosquitoes at sunset year-round. Always carry repellent on hikes here.

Fees and permits: Entrance fee of $20 per vehicle; permit valid for 7 days. Check the website in "Trail contacts" for information on passes, free entrance days, and dates closed. Ask about any available brochures for the trails.

Trail contact: Canaveral National Seashore Headquarters, 308 Julia St., Titusville 32796; (321) 267-1110. Also 7611 South Atlantic Ave., New Smyrna Beach 32169; (386) 428-3384. Visitor information recorded message, (321) 867-0677; nps.gov/cana/planyourvisit/hiking.htm.

Schedule: Open 6 a.m. year-round; closes 8 p.m. Apr through Oct, 6 p.m. Nov through Mar. The visitor information center is open 9 a.m. to 5 p.m. daily except Christmas. The visitor center is located on the right, a little over a mile south of the entrance gate kiosk.

Dog-friendly: Leashed pets allowed on trails but not on the beach

Trail surface: Dirt, oyster shells, and sand. The Turtle Mound Trail is mostly boardwalk but with significant inclines.

Land status: National seashore

Nearest town: New Smyrna Beach

Other trail users: Nature watchers, anglers

Water availability: Try the visitor center; best to bring your own

Maps: Provided at the entrance

Special considerations: Parking areas 1 through 5 have wheelchair-accessible entries onto the beach and accessible parking spaces located in front of each ramp. The ramps are flush with the parking lot and range from completely flat to a slight incline.

Amenities: Visitor center and restrooms are wheelchair accessible. The boardwalk trail leading to the top of Turtle Mound requires assistance. A beach wheelchair may be available from the visitor center, maximum 2-hour use.

Cell service: Wi-Fi available at the Apollo Beach Visitor Center. Cell service is generally good at this end of the national seashore.

Trail conditions: The inclines on the Turtle Mound boardwalk may be slippery following rain. The Eldora Hammock Trail has protruding roots in some places. You'll want to carry bug repellent on all trails here, although you may not need it.

Finding the trailhead: Apollo Beach is at the northern end of the Canaveral National Seashore. It is located 7 miles south of New Smyrna Beach, about midway on between Daytona Beach and Melbourne on Florida's East Coast .

From I-95, Florida's major East Coast highway, take exit 249 onto SR 44 toward DeLand/New Smyrna Beach. Go east to New Smyrna Beach (about 20 miles). Just before the main downtown area, watch for the junction of SR 44 with Canal Street and Lytle Avenue. Turn right onto Lytle Avenue, which becomes SR A1A and the South Causeway that crosses over the Halifax River. Follow SR A1A for 9 miles south of New Smyrna Beach to the National Seashore's north entrance at Apollo Beach. Trailhead GPS: Apollo Beach Entrance Station: 28.9368 / -80.8302; Apollo Visitor Center: 28.9271 / -80.8244

2 Turtle Mound Boardwalk Hike

Distance: 0.5-mile round-trip

Finding the trailhead: Located 0.96 mile from the seashore entrance kiosk. Park on the right shoulder in the designated area, and take the boardwalk inland toward the Indian River. Although the boardwalk is considered accessible, someone in a wheelchair will require assistance going up and down the steep inclines. Trailhead GPS: 28.930465 / -80.825697

The Hike

Turtle Mound is an ancient hillock of oyster shells left by the Timucua Indians. A 0.25-mile boardwalk leads to the top of the 2-acre shell pile. Bring bug spray; mosquitoes can be a bother.

It's been estimated that it took a million and a half bushels of oyster shells to create this site. The oyster-eating Timucua are credited with making the shell pile between 600 and 1400 CE. At 50 feet high, this is one of the tallest shell mounds remaining on Florida's east coast. The mound, possibly a high-ground refuge during hurricanes, extends more than 600 feet along the Indian River shoreline.

At one time the trail was built on the mound itself. Today the boardwalk protects the shells from being trod upon or picked over by souvenir hunters. The lack of foot traffic has allowed foliage to largely obscure parts of the site.

The midden potentially contains a treasure trove of artifacts, making it one of the more important archaeological site sites on Florida's east coast. It has never undergone a full archaeological excavation. Instead, the plan is to protect it for future scientists to uncover more information about the Timucua. Apparently, there is not enough interest and/or funding to do it now.

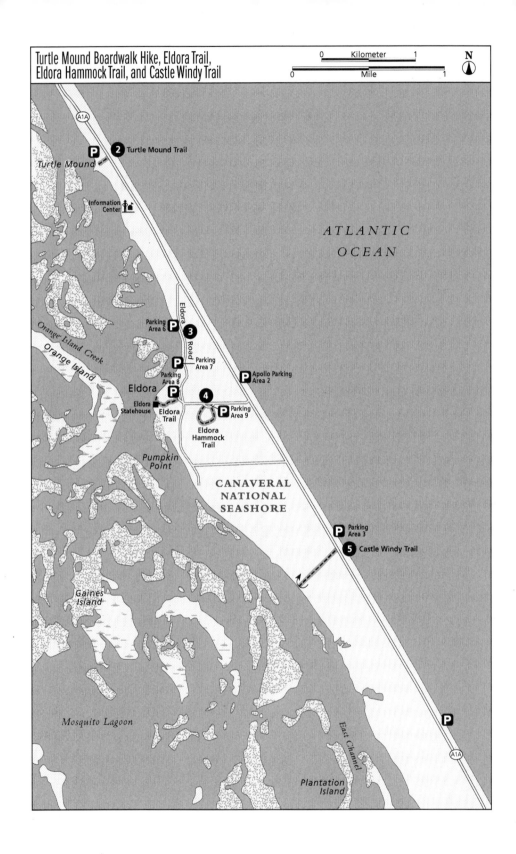

Turtle Mound Boardwalk Hike, Eldora Trail,
Eldora Hammock Trail, and Castle Windy Trail

Kilometer
0   1

Mile
0   1

N

A1A

P 2 Turtle Mound Trail

Turtle Mound

Information
Center

ATLANTIC
OCEAN

Orange Island Creek

Orange Island

Parking
Area 6 P

Eldora Road

3

Parking
Area 7

P Apollo Parking
Area 2

P
Parking
Area 8

Eldora

P

4

P Parking
Area 9

Eldora
Statehouse

Eldora
Trail

Eldora
Hammock
Trail

*Pumpkin
Point*

CANAVERAL
NATIONAL
SEASHORE

P Parking
Area 3

5 Castle Windy Trail

*Gaines
Island*

Mosquito Lagoon

East Channel

P

A1A

*Plantation
Island*

THE MOUND BUILDERS

Turtle Mound is an Indian midden-a trash heap of discarded shells accumulated over 600 years. A short boardwalk trail leads to the summit of the mound. Along the way, trailside signs explain the life-style of the Timucuan Indians. The Timucuan people inhabited this area living on the abundant marine resources of Mosquito Lagoon. The successive layers of shells are a record of the Timucuan culture. Please help preserve the archaeological history of the mound by staying on the boardwalk and leaving all natural and historic features as they are.

A Timucuan

Sherds Broken Shell Pick
...eological artifacts are
...historical record of
...ucuan life.

The story of the Turtle Mound builders

The Timucua hunted and fished along the coast for about 2,000 years. An estimated 40,000 of them were living in the region when the first Spanish settlers arrived. Their population was so dramatically reduced that most of the remaining Timucua fled the state when the Spanish temporarily withdrew from Florida in 1763.

Interpretive signs at several points on the trail explain the Timucua lifestyle in detail. On the top of the mound is a large viewing platform that offers a good view of the Indian River from the seashore's highest point. The mound of oyster and clam shells is not easily visible due to the fairly dense plant growth that has planted deep roots into this archeological site.

Miles and Directions

0.0 Start the hike on the boardwalk.

0.03 Go straight on the boardwalk.

0.14 The boardwalk makes a T; go right.

0.25 Reach the platform at the top overlooking the Indian River. Looking north, it offers a fine view of Mosquito Lagoon. When ready, make your return to the parking lot.

0.27 A handrail is available on the steep incline.

0.4 Go left on the boardwalk to return to the parking lot.

0.5 Arrive back at the parking lot.

3 Eldora Trail

Distance: 0.5-mile round-trip

Finding the trailhead: Follow SR A1A about 1.9 miles from the seashore entrance to where the road makes a Y. Turn right onto the one-way Eldora Road. The hiking trail starts at parking lot 6, the southern end of the first parking lot, near the kiosk and restrooms. The path is packed sand that could be difficult for a wheelchair. Trailhead GPS: 28.915408 / -80.818154

The Hike

The trail first goes straight through a hammock by the Indian River and then joins El Dora Loop Road. Pass a small public fishing pier on the Indian River and arrive at the El Dora trailhead. Go right and follow the short trail from Parking Lot 8 to the impressive white wooden building called the Eldora State House at the river shoreline. The old building is open to the public and listed on the National Register of Historic Places. It is a storehouse of exhibits and information about those who lived in the thriving town of Eldora between 1877 and 1914.

The vanished town of Eldora is typical of many small villages that for a time thrived with scores of people—perhaps as many as 200. A shallow-draft steamboat frequently stopped to take on such goods as honey and saw palmetto berries to be used for medicinal purposes. In 1895 a freeze killed the orange crop and the town began its decline as people moved away.

Only about ten people, mostly fishermen, lived there when the National Park Service took over the property in 1975. Today you can use the dock in front of the State House to fish in the Indian River if you have a Florida saltwater license.

Miles and Directions

0.0 Start at trail kiosk on parking lot 6 and enter a thick hammock on a wide sandy path beside the Indian River that leads to parking lot 7.

0.13 Pass a small on the right before arriving at parking lot 8. Go right to follow the trail toward the Indian River. (**Option:** Start the hike from here.) Pass a small fishing pier on the right before arriving at parking lot 8. Go right to follow the trail toward the Indian River and the Eldora State House. (**Option:** Start the hike from here.)

0.25 Arrive at the Eldora State House. Afterward, retrace your steps, or visit the fishing pier on the way back.

0.5 Arrive back at Eldora Loop Road parking lot 6.

4 Eldora Hammock Trail

Distance: 0.45-mile loop

Finding the trailhead: As you leave the parking lot on the Eldora Loop Trail, follow the road as it curves left and soon arrive at the Eldora Hammock Trail, on the right. Turn into the trail's parking lot. The trail surface is soft sand and not accessible for a normal wheelchair. Trailhead GPS: 28.908793 / -80.815722

The Hike

This 0.45-mile loop trail can be a good location for early-morning birding. The hike goes through a thick coastal forest where mosquitoes can be fierce, and in places the infrequently used trail may be clogged with golden silk spiderwebs. The large speckled spiders are harmless, not a reason to avoid this pretty little hike. The short trail is nicely shaded by thick cover, and the interpretive markers are quite good. The path of soft sand may take some getting used to.

Miles and Directions

0.0 Start from the parking lot.
0.03 Pass two large oaks on the right side of the trail.
0.04 The trail makes a sharp right.
0.11 Pass several large cut logs.
0.4 Return to the parking lot.
0.45 Arrive back at the parking lot.

5 Castle Windy Trail

Distance: 0.7 mile out and back

Finding the trailhead: The southernmost walk at Apollo Beach begins at parking area 3 on SR A1A. The trail starts on the opposite side of the road, on the Indian River side of SR A1A. The trail surface is soft sand and not accessible for a regular wheelchair. Trailheads GPS: 28.8985 / -80.8035

The Hike

This short straight trail crosses from a beach bordering the Atlantic to Mosquito Lagoon, part of the Indian River. An interpretive brochure available from the north end visitor center explains the coastal vegetation and how it has adapted to wind and salt spray coming off the Atlantic.

In a relatively short space, this trail has more than a dozen identification stops demonstrating how plants are divided into distinct zones based on soil, moisture, and exposure to ocean breezes. For instance, the live oak trees here are pruned by salt-laden winds that kill the bud ends and restrict the trees' upward growth. Farther inland, this effect is lessened and trees grow taller.

At the end of the walk, reach a midden (shell mound) near the shore of the Indian River. Like the one at Turtle Mound, it was built by the Timucua Indians. Called Castle Windy, the shells and other objects from the midden have been dated to 1,000 CE. Castle Windy's midden is largely unprotected. No climbing or souvenir taking is permitted.

Miles and Directions

0.0 Cross SR A1A and join the marked trail. Go straight.

0.14 Pass a bench on the left. Continue straight.

0.3 Reach the shell mound. Go straight.

0.35 Arrive at the shore of Mosquito Lagoon and the Indian River with a small cleared area and a picnic table. This is the end of the hike; retrace your steps.

0.7 Arrive back at parking area 3.

More Information

Lifeguards are on duty at Canaveral National Seashore from Memorial Day through Labor Day. Park visitors can join a ranger to watch a loggerhead sea turtle nest on the beach in June and July. Reservations are taken on May 1 for June programs and on June 1 for July programs. Call (321) 867-4077 or (386) 428-3384, ext. 10.

Honeymoon Island State Park

In addition to miles of white sand beach, Honeymoon Island has more than 5 miles of hiking trails. Many people visit here simply to take the boat ride to nearby Caladesi Island, hike 8. Honeymoon Island deserves better than that.

Honeymoon Island didn't exist before 1921. It was part of Caladesi Island, a large land area known as Hog Island. In 1921, a hurricane turned Caladesi into two separate islands. A New York developer purchased the newly created island in 1939, changed its name to Honeymoon Island, and built fifty palm-thatched bungalows to match the honeymoon theme and made the place famous until World War II. Honeymoon Island lost its romantic allure during the war when it was turned into a getaway for tired war production workers, and the resort island went into decline.

More development efforts took place when a causeway was built in 1964 to connect Honeymoon Island to the mainland. All such plans ended when a 1970 environmental impact study stopped further dredging and filling. The state purchased the land in 1974.

Now attracting more than a million visitors a year, Honeymoon Island has become one of Florida's most popular state parks. Its 4 miles of beach attracts people who want to play in the sun as well as those who just want to sit and watch the sun go down at the end of each day.

Start: End of the north parking lot

Distance: 2.5 miles for the longest trail; also almost 5 miles of nature trails to choose from.

Difficulty: Easy

Hiking time: 1.5–2.5 hours

Trail surface: Natural, mostly sand

Seasons: Nov to June for most comfortable hiking weather

Fees and permits: $8 per vehicle; $4 sunset entry fee

Trail contact: Honeymoon Island State Park, 1 Causeway Blvd., Dunedin 34698; (727) 241-6106; floridastateparks.org/honeymoonisland

Schedule: Open daily, 8 a.m. until sunset

Dog-friendly: Dogs allowed at the pet beach on the island's southern tip and on the Nature Trail if on a 6-foot handheld leash

Trail surface: Dirt, sand

Land status: Florida state park

Nearest town: Dunedin

Other trail users: Nature lovers, pet owners

Water availability: Restroom facilities, concession stand

Maps: Available at the park

Special considerations: This is a favorite spot for watching the sun disappear into the Gulf of Mexico. Accessible amenities include the Rotary Centennial Nature Center, elevated boardwalks to the beach, concession with food and gift store, picnic facilities with tables and grills, parking, and restrooms.

Amenities: Just about everything you could want to do at a beach. Activities include picnicking, surfing, swimming, cycling, and paddling. Rental kayaks, chairs, and umbrellas are available.

Cell service: Good in all locations

Trail conditions: The Osprey Trail is high and dry. However, the Pelican Trail is sometimes wet enough near its end that you may want to take a side trail to return to the Osprey Trail and exit from there. Have bug repellent ready.

On Honeymoon Island's Osprey Trail, look for the fish hawk with a distinctive brown band across its eye.

6 Osprey and Pelican Cove Trails

Distance: 2.5-mile loop

Finding the trailhead: Honeymoon Island State Park Area is located at the extreme west end of SR 586, north of Dunedin. Follow SR 586 to cross the Dunedin Causeway to Honeymoon Island State Park. The trailhead for the Osprey Trail is accessed from the northern end of the northernmost parking lot. Trailhead GPS: 28.068423 / -82.830228

The Hike

The Osprey and Pelican hike leads through one of the last remaining stands of South Florida virgin slash pine. The two connecting trails form the Osprey Loop Trail and also parallel each other. The trailhead is at the Osprey Trail.

The Osprey Trail is named for the many osprey nests found along this coastline. Oystercatchers, snowy plovers, and least terns also nest in the area. Roseate spoonbills, snowy egrets, great blue herons, and many other species frequently feed in the bay and estuaries. Gopher tortoises and armadillos are often seen here as well. But beware of the poison ivy also found near the trails.

OSPREYS

Often mistaken for the bald eagle, the American osprey is frequently found in its company since the two fish hawks often share the same territory, yet an osprey is but a small shadow of America's national symbol. A more compact bird, it is only 22 to 25 inches in length compared to the bald eagle's loftier 35 inches. However, its wings are unusually long for its size, extending 55 to 73 inches.

What frequently accounts for the confusion between an osprey and a bald eagle is that both birds are brown and white. However, their color patterns are very different and easy to distinguish.

Where both the head and tail feathers of a bald eagle are an unmistakable white, the upper and tail feathers of the osprey are colored. The osprey has a distinct brown band through its eye and on the side of its face, which easily marks it as different from a bald eagle.

In the Southeast, wherever there are water and fish, the osprey is almost always present. The osprey prefers to nest in the limbs of dead trees, on top of channel markers, or atop telephone or electrical transmission poles. The nests are tall and wide, made of sticks, and reused year after year. Ospreys add to their nests each season, so a long-used nest tends to be huge.

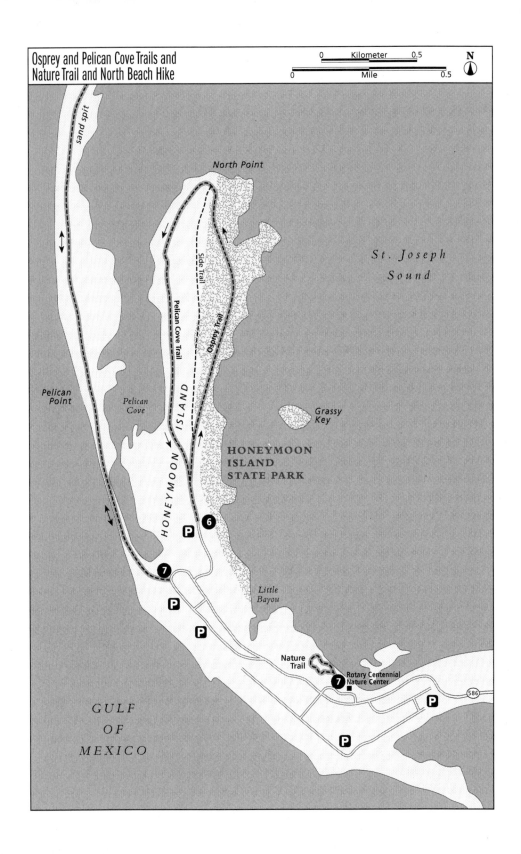

Osprey and Pelican Cove Trails and
Nature Trail and North Beach Hike

Kilometer
0   0.5
0   0.5
Mile

N

sand spit

North Point

St. Joseph
Sound

Side Trail

Pelican Cove Trail

Osprey Trail

Pelican
Point

Pelican
Cove

HONEYMOON ISLAND

Grassy
Key

HONEYMOON
ISLAND
STATE PARK

P   6

P   7

Little
Bayou

P

P

Nature
Trail

Rotary Centennial
Nature Center

7

586

P

GULF

OF

MEXICO

P

Since it is sheltered by a sand spit, the 0.75-mile-long Pelican Cove Trail can provide excellent bird observation on windy days. The northern portion of the island usually affords good open-water views of shorebirds; see Nature Trails (hike 7) below.

Mangroves line much of the Pelican Cove Trail, making insect repellent a good idea. Shade is sparse; wear a hat and use sunblock. Two observation decks provide good bird viewing at low tide.

Ideally, you will make this walk as a loop. Sometimes, however, the Pelican Cove Trail can be wet at high tide, and you may want to take one of the side trails that heads east and links with the drier Osprey Trail.

Miles and Directions

0.0 Start at the northern end of the parking lot. Go right onto the Osprey Trail.

0.5 Mile marker; keep to the right.

1.0 A kiosk explains the osprey's fishing techniques.

1.1 Join the Pelican Cove Trail.

1.6 Junction from the left offers the option to rejoin the drier Osprey Trail. Assuming conditions are dry enough, continue ahead to stay on Pelican Cove Trail.

1.9 The trail climbs uphill to rejoin the Osprey Trail. Go right to return to the parking lot.

2.5 Arrive back at the parking lot.

7 Nature Trail and North Beach Hike

Distance: Nature Trail: 0.25-mile loop; North Beach Hike: 5 miles out and back

Finding the trailhead: Honeymoon Island State Park is located at the extreme west end of SR 586, north of Dunedin. Follow SR 586 to cross the Dunedin Causeway to Honeymoon Island State Park. The Rotary Centennial Nature Center is the first right past the park entrance. Nature Center trailhead GPS: 28.060296 / -82.822690; North Beach trailhead GPS: 28.064589 / -82.833056

The Hikes

The Rotary Centennial Nature Center features a 0.25-mile loop trail along mangroves close to the seawall overlooking St. Joseph Sound. Low tide is best for a good view of shorebirds, including oystercatchers and hunting osprey skimming the water. Dolphins or even a shark could appear. In addition to mangroves, there is a mix of cabbage palms, southern red cedar trees, and sea grapes, with a few slash pines mixed in.

The North Beach hike is a 5.0 mile out-and-back hike on the sand spit forming North Beach. For a hike of about 2.5 hours round-trip, start from the trailhead at the northern parking lot. Due to the intense sun and the glare off the water, you'll want

A modified walking pole should provide more stability in sand.

good sun protection. You could have a breeze that keeps warm-weather hiking from turning unpleasant. Make this hike at low tide. No dogs are allowed on the beach.

The beach is a little rocky at the beginning for about 0.25 mile. This is the lingering remains of a developer's dredging before the land became a state park.

The sand soon spreads out wide and smooth. On the walk, you never really see the end of the beach because the shoreline is constantly turning right.

Look for white-clawed ghost crabs and hopefully plenty of seashells. The best shelling is after winter storms. Birds you might see here are plovers, sandpipers, gulls, oystercatchers, pelicans, terns, and skimmers. A dolphin sighting is a distinct possibility. Any sea turtle nests here are fenced off and should not be disturbed. If you decide to walk in the water, shuffle your feet to scare off any stingrays.

Update: Erosion and sand migration have separated the northernmost mile of Honeymoon Island State Park from the main island. Do not venture into the water and attempt to cross the channel due to the possibility of deep water and current. This may only be temporary.

Caladesi Island State Park

Located 3 miles offshore in the Gulf of Mexico, Caladesi Island is one of Florida's largest undeveloped barrier islands. Its magnificent beach has been included on the "America's Best Beaches" list six times since 2002. It ranked as number 1 in the entire nation in 2008. The sands here are indeed extra fine.

As Caladesi Island is reached only by boat, this is one of the state's more remote hiking trails. Fortunately, you don't need your own craft to get here. A scheduled ferry travels frequently from nearby Honeymoon Island State Park. Rough sea conditions sometimes prevent the ferry from running. Call ahead whenever it's windy to confirm the ferry schedule. Those with a small boat can stay overnight at Caladesi Island's 108-slip marina or anchor offshore.

Start: Kiosk on the Caladesi Island dock
Distance: 3.0 miles
Difficulty: Easy
Hiking time: 1.5-2 hours
Seasons: Mar and Apr tend to be windy. Pay attention to temperatures throughout the year. It can be chilly at times.
Fees and permits: Entrance fee of $8 per vehicle (2-8 people.). Vehicles stay at Honeymoon Island. The ferry ride from the park is $18 for adults, $9 for kids 6-12; children under 5 are free. A military discount is available for active duty and retired personnel with valid ID, which also applies to the holder's companions.
Trail contact: Caladesi Island State Park, 1 Causeway Blvd., Dunedin 34698; (727) 469-5918; floridastateparks.org/caladesiisland
Schedule: Open daily, sunrise to sunset. The ferry from Honeymoon Island State Park to Caladesi Island leaves hourly beginning at 10 a.m. The last ferry is at 3 p.m. The stay on Caladesi Island is limited to 4 hours. To contact the ferry service, call (727) 734-1501. Ferry schedule is subject to change.

The Beach Trail at Caladesi Island State Park takes you to one of the nation's top beaches.

Dog-friendly: Pets are not permitted on the ferry from Honeymoon Island. Pets brought to the island by private boat must be leashed and are not allowed on the beach. Owners must provide proof of rabies vaccination and keep their animal confined to a designated area.

Trail surface: Sand and boardwalks

Land status: Florida state park

Nearest town: Dunedin

Other trail users: Nature watchers

Water availability: Restrooms, concession stand

Maps: Available at entrance

Amenities: Bathhouses have restrooms. Beach chairs, beach umbrellas, and kayaks are available for rental; picnic tables and grills also provided. Accessible facilities include the ferry from Honeymoon Island, elevated boardwalks to the beach, picnic facilities with tables and grills, Caladesi Café, and the park restrooms. Beach wheelchairs are available for free. Inquire at the ranger station.

Cell service: Good

Trail conditions: Rain may cause possibly slick boardwalk areas. The terrain is mostly flat and sandy in some areas. Have bug repellent handy.

8 The Island Trail

Distance: 3.0-mile loop

Finding the trailhead: The hiking trailhead is at the kiosk on the dock where the ferry lands.

Coming east from Orlando, take I-4 West to I-275, then go south to SR 60 West. Cross the Courtney Campbell Causeway, then turn right onto US 19 North. Go left on Curlew Road (SR 586). Follow SR 586 and cross the Dunedin Causeway to arrive at Honeymoon Island State Park.

From north of Tampa, take I-75 South to I-275 South to the Hillsborough Avenue exit. Go west to a slight left at Curlew Road (SR 586). Pass a fork at SR 580. Follow SR 586 to cross the Dunedin Causeway to Honeymoon Island State Park.

From south of Tampa, take I-75 North to I-275 North to the Roosevelt Avenue exit. (Follow signs for St. Petersburg–Clearwater International Airport, the last exit before the Howard Franklin Bridge.) Stay right on SR 686 West when SR 688 forks to the left. Next, turn right (north) onto McMullen Booth Road (CR 611) to cross the Bayside Bridge. Go left on Curlew Road (SR 586). Follow SR 586, crossing the Dunedin Causeway, to Honeymoon Island State Park. Trailhead GPS: 28.032691 / -82.81926

The Hike

From the Caladesi Island dock, a boardwalk leads to a pair of hikes. One is the shorter beach trail offering 2 miles of gorgeous waterfront walking beside the Gulf in open sun. To access this walk, follow the designated boardwalk from the ferry dock to the Gulf beach. Long and beautiful, Caladesi Island's beach has been ranked one of the best in the United States, including Hawaii. Understandably, it is crowded here on weekends. Rental umbrellas and picnic pavilions offer some of the best beachfront shade.

The boardwalk starting behind the cafe also provides access to the 3.0-mile Island Trail. The trail loops mostly through the interior but also visits the beach. The interior is a closed maritime hammock formed by red bay, sabal palm, live oak, and southern

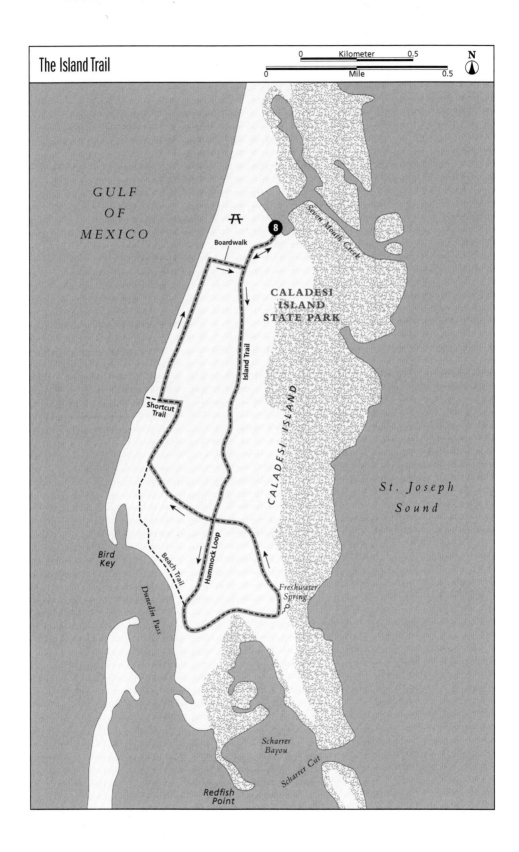

The Island Trail

0 Kilometer 0.5

0 Mile 0.5

N

GULF

OF

MEXICO

Boardwalk

8

Seven Mouth Creek

CALADESI
ISLAND
STATE PARK

Island Trail

Shortcut
Trail

CALADESI ISLAND

St. Joseph
Sound

Bird
Key

Hammock Loop

Beach Trail

Dunedin Pass

Freshwater
Spring

Scharrer
Bayou

Redfish
Point

Scharrer Cut

red cedar. Woodland residents you could encounter include marsh rabbits, armadillos, raccoons, and squirrels.

Start the Island Trail by bearing left on the boardwalk and going straight. The trail wanders through a scrub forest then passes large salt-tolerant bushes like sea myrtle, a woody plant that can remove salt through its leaves. In fall these plants may be covered with tiny white cloudlike flowers. Another hardy salt-tolerant species along this walk is the sand live oak. Its leaves are curled, a feature that allows the trees to survive in Caladesi Island's salty environment.

Remaining on the Island Trail, you'll soon come upon Hammock Loop. The trail also takes you into a stand of Florida's last remaining virgin slash pine. At 1.3 miles, pass a spring of fresh water, the island's largest freshwater source. This spring is what allowed Swiss immigrant Henry Scharrer, arriving in 1883, to survive on what was then known as Hog Island for almost fifty years.

Hog Island was greatly reduced by a hurricane in 1921. It ripped Hog Island apart and replaced it with an open-water area now known as Hurricane Pass. The one big island was replaced by two smaller ones: Hog Island, now named Honeymoon Island, and the new Caladesi Island. The name Caladesi is said to mean "beautiful bayou" in Spanish.

Skirting the salt marshes, Hammock Loop connects to the longer Beach Trail that leads down to the exceptionally fine beach. The dune line, populated with sea oats and sea purslane (also called sea pickle), is a favorite nesting area for both sea turtles and birds. Leaving the beach, the trail returns to the boardwalk. The hike ends at the boat dock.

Miles and Directions

- **0.0** Start on the boardwalk leading to the Gulf; go left to join the marked Island Trail.
- **0.2** Pass the anti-litter kiosk. Take an interpretive brochure for the trails then go straight.
- **0.6** Ignore the shortcut sign to the beach, which you will visit later. Go straight to see the old-growth forest on the Hammock Loop.
- **1.0** Junction with the Hammock Loop; go left.
- **1.3** Pass a freshwater spring on the right.
- **1.8** The Hammock Loop ends. Turn right onto the Island Trail, then go left to join the Beach Trail. Continue west.
- **2.0** A shortcut trail comes in from the right. Ignore it and go straight. Prepare for the trail to make a sharp left.
- **2.5** Arrive at the first boardwalk, going inland and crossing the dunes. Follow the boardwalk, going right.
- **2.8** Reach the junction with the Island Trail and the access boardwalk that leads back to the dock; turn left.
- **3.0** Arrive back at the ferry dock.

Lake Woodruff National Wildlife Refuge

This 21,574-acre refuge offers some of the state's best waterfowl viewing, thanks in part to a series of impoundments encompassing three large pond-size pools. The refuge is also a good place for a family outing. The open-water pools are popular for fishing. Local residents often bring folding chairs and ice chests and spend the day. A Florida fishing license is required.

The refuge has more than 20 miles of hiking trails that offer the opportunity to view some of its diverse wildlife. The walks vary in length from a 0.5-mile loop walk to the featured hike, a 6.0-mile round-trip trail to Pontoon Landing.

The three impoundment pools attract alligators, hawks, deer, otters, and numerous species of songbirds. In winter, when blue-winged teal and ring-necked ducks are common, they are particularly good for birding. In spring, wood ducks and their new broods attract much of the attention. Other birds normally found here include white ibis, little blue herons, great blue herons, and great egrets.

The refuge's hardwood swamp, freshwater marsh, and pinewoods house a large variety of creatures, including Florida black bears, bald eagles, otters, egrets, herons, and alligators. Bobcats and foxes live on the preserve, but you would be extremely fortunate to see one.

Check out the Audubon observation tower, located 0.75 mile from the parking area. It has a fixed binocular for a good overview of the impoundments and marshes.

Be sure to check out the Audubon observation tower and spotting scope overlooking several pools at Lake Woodruff National Wildlife Refuge.

Pontoon Landing Hike and Nature Trails

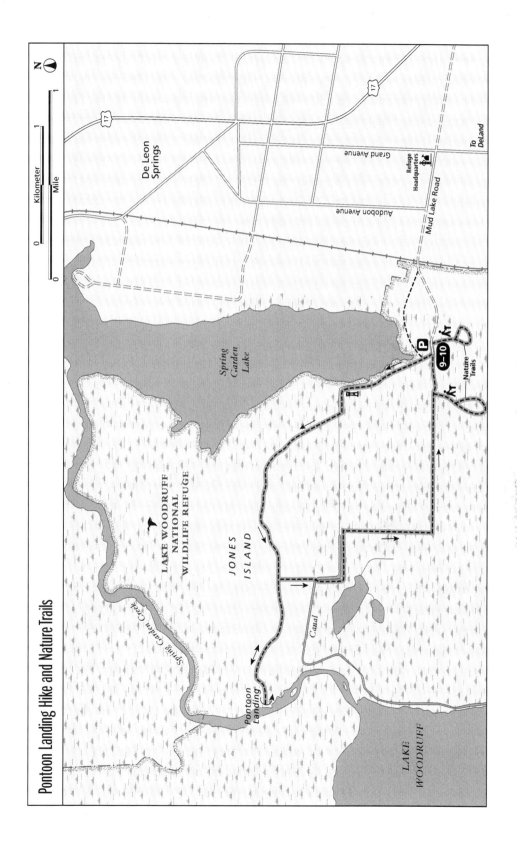

Start: Live Oak parking lot off Mud Lake Road

Distance: Includes hikes around three impoundment pools of varying size. The longest berm is 2.4 miles. Other hikes include the featured 6.0-mile out-and-back hike to Pontoon Island and the 0.6-mile Volusia Tract. All trails link together and offer a good day's walking.

Difficulty: Easy except for sun exposure

Hiking time: 2–3 hours, depending on chosen trails

Seasons: Dec through Mar for the coolest weather and the best birding

Fees and permits: No fees or permits required for normal day use

Trail contact: Lake Woodruff National Wildlife Refuge, 2045 Mud Lake Rd., De Leon Springs 32130; (386) 985-4673; fws.gov/refuge/lake -woodruff (*Note:* The refuge office may be open on weekdays only.)

Schedule: The refuge is open daily, sunrise to sunset. Visitor center hours vary by season and whether there is staff to operate it: Nov to Mar, 8 a.m. to 4:30 p.m. daily; Apr through Oct, 8 a.m. to 4:30 p.m., Mon to Fri only; closed weekends and federal holidays. If using the visitor center facilities is important to you, call ahead to see if the building is open.

Dog-friendly: Pets prohibited

Trail surface: Dirt, grass paths, and boardwalk

Land status: National wildlife refuge

Nearest town: De Leon Springs

Other trail users: Anglers, nature watchers, cyclists

Water availability: At the restroom, if it is open; best to bring your own

Maps: Available at the refuge office or online at fws.gov/refuge/lake-woodruff/visit-us/trails. Click "View Details" for individual maps of each hike.

Special considerations: This is an open area with little shade. Bring a hat, sunscreen, lots of water, and insect repellent.

Amenities: Restroom available near the Live Oak trailhead if the NWR has enough staff. Visitor center and nature store may be open between Nov and June from 9 a.m. to 4:30 p.m., Mon through Sat. Call ahead to make certain the center and store are open when you want to visit.

Cell service: Good

Trail conditions: Usually high and dry around the three pools. Following heavy rains, call ahead to learn their status. A tropical storm may close the refuge due to area flooding. This is a place where you'll always want to have sun protection and bug repellent handy.

⑨ Pontoon Landing Hike

Distance: 6.0 miles round-trip

Finding the trailhead: From the city of DeLand, go north on SR 17 to De Leon Springs. From SR 17 turn west onto Wheeler or Retta Street to reach Grand Avenue. Go south on Grand Avenue to Mud Lake Road and turn west onto Mud Lake Road. The refuge quarters will be on your right. Keep straight (west) on Mud Lake Road. Trailhead GPS: 29.106880 / -81.370998

The Hike

Several hikes are available. Probably the most popular is the stroll around some or all of the water impoundment pools that become visible after you leave the parking lot. The shortest perimeter walk is around Pool 1, a distance of 1.52 miles. Pool 2, the largest, has a perimeter of 2.34 miles. Its northern perimeter enters a pine forest, where you'll find some shade.

The smallest is Pool 3, with a perimeter of 1.27 miles sandwiched under Pool 2. Hiking the perimeters of the three pools totals 5.3 miles. Except for a section of Pool 2, the impoundments are in the open with no shade. In dry weather, walking atop the earthen dikes on a grassy path is a nice casual hike until the sun comes out. A hat, sunblock, and bug repellent are essential.

In addition to circumnavigating the three pools, you can hike to Pontoon Landing by following an out-and-back trail from Pool 2. The trail goes through Jones Island and a pine forest, offering some welcome shade. The hike ends at Pontoon Landing on Spring Garden Creek.

Miles and Directions

0.0 Start at the refuge parking lot and go north on the Pool 1 impoundment path.

0.75 Reach the wildlife observation tower. Walk northwest on the outer edge of Pool 2 and enter Jones Island's pine forest with scattered shade.

2.25 Junction with the 0.81-mile Pontoon Island Trail as the Pool 2 impoundment perimeter turns south. The Pontoon Island Trail also enjoys some shade.

3.0 Arrive at Garden Creek and Pontoon Landing, your turnaround point. Spring Garden Creek is fed by Spring Garden Lake at De Leon Springs State Park, located just north of the refuge.

3.81 Junction with Pool 2. You have the option to retrace your steps or extending the hike by walking new ground. For a change of scenery, turn south to walk a new section of Pool 2. When Pool 2 intersects Pool 3, join the new impoundment's path to complete your return to the trailhead. As you near the trailhead, the Hammock Nature Trail intersects your path from the right.

6.0 Arrive back at the refuge parking lot.

10 Nature Trails

Finding the trailhead: The refuge is near DeLand, 25 miles west of Daytona Beach. From DeLand, go north on SR 17 to De Leon Springs. From SR 17, turn west onto Wheeler or Retta Street to reach Grand Avenue. Go south on Grand Avenue to reach Mud Lake Road and turn west onto Mud Lake Road. The refuge quarters are on your right. Keep straight (west) on Mud Lake Road. Trailhead GPS: 29.106880 / -81.370998

The Hikes

The two nature trails near the trailhead are a nice contrast to the open pool walks. Both are well-shaded trails and travel through rich oak hammocks and saw palmetto. The shorter Live Oak Nature Trail is 0.5 mile long and begins from the Mud Lake Road parking lot. Portions of the Live Oak trail may be wet after heavy rains.

The 0.47-mile Hammock Nature Trail is located at the base of the Pool 3 impoundment. Reach the hike by walking straight from the parking lot and along the Pool 1 perimeter. The Hammock Trail is on your left.

Both trails feature live oaks, which keep their green leaves year-round, as do the saw palmetto trees also found here. The palmettos are named for the tiny razor edges along their leaves. Today, saw palmetto berries are one of the hottest herbal products on the market. An extract from them is promoted as a preventative against prostate cancer.

More Information

Several more hikes at Lake Woodruff NWR are located away from the pool impoundments. Starting near the parking lot is the **0.5-mile Green Tree Trail**, which accesses the **0.75-mile Myakka Trail**, located east of the parking lot.

The Myakka Trail can also be accessed by walking east on Mud Lake Road until you see a sign pointing to the trail. The Myakka Trail is laid out in the shape of a T and subdivided into four smaller loop walks by connector trails. A wildlife observation platform is located on the western perimeter of the Myakka Trail.

Eastside Trail: The trailhead for the Eastern Trail is on Mud Lake Road opposite the Myakka Trail. You should spot a sign for the trail on the left as you enter the WMA. The only hike of consequence is the linear out-and-back trail of 2.75 miles. The East Side Trail leads to the Volusia Tract (see below). The Eastside Trail hike expands to 3.27 miles if you hike the two small loops near the trailhead. Another option is to hike the perimeters of the two loops, which total less than a mile.

Volusia Tract: This 10.6-mile hike is accessed by taking the Eastside Trail or by vehicle from SR 44, also known as West New York Avenue. From SR 44, turn north onto North Shell Road to reach the Volusia Tract parking lot.

The Volusia Tract is subdivided into nineteen sections and too complicated to describe here. For more information, visit fws.gov/refuge/lake-woodruff/visit-us/trails and select the "Volusia Trail" map. Volusia is the name of the Florida county where Lake Woodruff is located.

Hontoon Island State Park

Hontoon may not be Robinson Crusoe's island, but in the mushrooming Central Florida region, it's the next best thing. Hontoon Island has no land access—visitors must arrive by the park's ferry or use a private boat. A Florida Park Service ferry runs every 15 minutes, taking visitors across the narrow river channel that separates the 1,650-acre park from the mainland. Stand on the dock to attract the boatman's attention if the ferry is on the other side.

The ferry runs from 8 a.m. until 1 hour before sunset, subject to change. It carries only people; the only motorized vehicles on the island belong to park personnel. The island's featured hike, the Hammock Hiking Nature Trail, leads to a huge Mayaca Indian shell midden made from many thousands (if not millions) of tiny snail shells left by generations of Mayaca, believed to have hunted and fished here for more than 12,000 years. The park museum provides information about these first inhabitants. The Mayaca differ from the Timucua, who built the famous shell mound at Canaveral National Seashore.

One of the outstanding natural features on Hontoon Island is a 500-year-old live oak tree at the end of the 1.7-mile Timucuan Trail Road.

Start: Marked trailhead to the right of the dock and behind the administrative offices

Distance: 3.0 miles out and back

Difficulty: Easy unless muddy areas

Hiking time: About 90 minutes if you take time to explore the shell mound and area around it

Seasons: Mid-November to May for the best weather

Fees and permits: No ferry or entrance fee, subject to change

Trail contact: Hontoon Island State Park, 2309 River Ridge Rd., DeLand 32720; (833) 953-2583; floridastateparks.org/parks-and-trails/hontoon-island-state-park

Schedule: Open 8 a.m. to 1 hour before sunset

Dog-friendly: Leashed pets permitted; check the park website for pet restrictions

Trail surface: Jeep road, natural surface

Land status: Florida state park

Nearest town: DeLand

Other trail users: Possibly cyclists

Water availability: Bring your own

Maps: Available at the park office and online at floridastateparks.org/sites/default/files/media/file/Hontoon_Island_Feb.2023.pdf

Special considerations: Accessible amenities include ferry service, picnic tables and grills, a cabin for an overnight stay, restrooms, and the visitor center/museum. The hike is not considered accessible.

Camping: Each of the 12 primitive campsites has a picnic table, ground grill, and access to nearby drinking water. No electricity is available. The restrooms have showers and flush toilets.

Amenities: Free ferry service, primitive camping, rustic cabins, playground, hiking, fishing, cycling, and picnicking

Cell service: Good

Trail conditions: This trail usually is an easy walk but wet in spots after rain. Ask park rangers about trail conditions prior to hiking. Have bug repellent handy, and be prepared for open sun.

You'll be lucky to see a river otter out of the water. All you usually see is the splash as it disappears underwater.

11 Hammock Hiking Nature Trail

Distance: 3 miles out and back

Finding the trailhead: Take US 17/92 to DeLand from I-4. Turn left onto SR 17. Stay on SR 17 for several miles before turning left onto SR 44. Go west and turn left onto CR 4110 (Old New York Avenue). Follow CR 4110 to CR 4125 (Hontoon Road) and make a left onto River Ridge Road. Continue to the parking area for the park and ferry launch. The ferry is at Hontoon Island Adventures, 2309 River Ridge Rd., DeLand. Trailhead GPS: 28.974522 / -81.357743

The Hike

First, a sales pitch for Hontoon Island: This is a terrific place for a family weekend. You can camp in a primitive setting or opt for the cottages that come virtually complete except for bedding and food. Plan meals for here carefully—there are no stores on the island. What you come without, you do without.

When you arrive on the island, note the large owl totem pole near the dock, a replica of a Mayaca Indian totem pole found in the park. The original totem, made from a single tree, was dredged up in 1955 from deep muck that protected it for an estimated 600 years. This was a remarkable find: the only totem pole ever discovered in the entire Southeast.

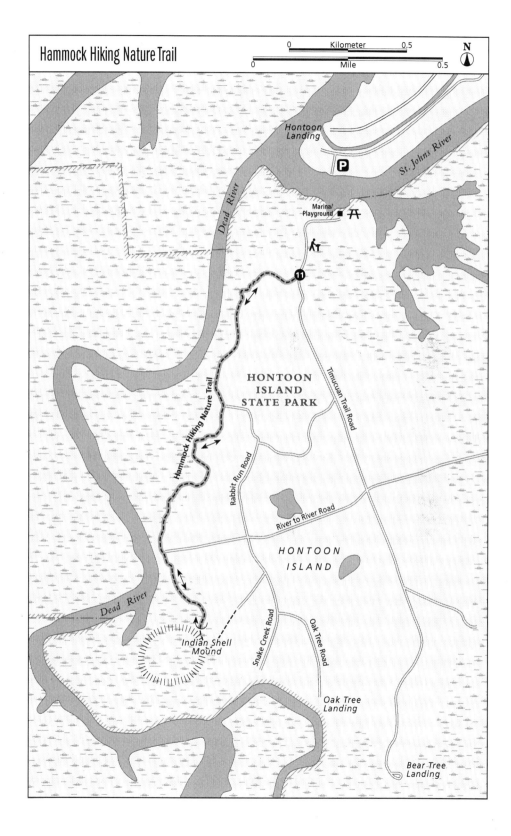

Hammock Hiking Nature Trail

One archaeologist called it the largest wooden effigy ever recovered from a North American archaeological site. Two smaller wood carvings were also discovered. They depicted an otter holding a fish and a bird resembling a pelican. One theory about the totem is that it was used to identify the Myacca clan living here.

The totem from Hontoon island is now located at the Timucuan Ecological and Historic Preserve at Fort Caroline National Monument, near the mouth of the St. Johns River east of Jacksonville. The Mayaca hopefully will have a center of their own one day.

The marked trailhead for the Hammock Hiking Nature Trail begins to the right of the dock and behind the administrative offices. The walk itself takes about 90 minutes round-trip, passing first through a slash pine forest and then descending near Hontoon Dead River, a tributary of the St. Johns. The island is a mix of swamps, marshes, pine flatwoods, and oak hammocks. The trail ends at the massive mound of snail shells near Hontoon Dead River.

The midden is 300 feet long, 100 feet wide, and 35 five feet high. The shells accumulated over many hundreds if not thousands of years to form the large mound. Other shell middens are located along the island's shoreline.

As at Turtle Mound at Canaveral National Seashore, this shell pile is believed to have been used either ceremonially or as a trash heap. It may also have served as safe high ground during hurricanes. There are several small islands made totally of ancient shell mounds.

Miles and Directions

0.0 Start at the trailhead for the Nature Trail at a sign behind the administrative offices.

1.3 Pass a bench for a first view of the Dead River.

1.5 Arrive at the Mayaca shell midden. When ready, retrace your steps through the forest.

3.0 Arrive back at the Nature Trail sign.

Blue Spring State Park

The West Indian manatee is believed to be the basis of the mermaid legend because of its humanlike face and broad tail like that of a beaver. Manatees, which may weigh as much as a ton, eat up to 100 pounds of vegetation every day. The mammals once ranged from North Carolina to Texas, but destruction of their habitat through development and pollution has drastically reduced their population. Only Florida has a resident manatee population, which is believed to number somewhere between 5,000 and 6,000 animals.

The manatee, originally a four-footed land creature, is considered a close relative of the elephant. It has no natural enemies, although human progress has endangered their chances for survival. Seagrass, a staple in the manatee diet, is disappearing due to nutrient runoff and environmental damage.

Manatees cannot survive in water colder than 68°F. They flee the neighboring St. Johns River for the warmer 72°F temperature of Blue Spring run. The boardwalk beside the spring run offers the remarkable view of as many as 700 animals lazing in the clear spring water.

Nowhere else in the world is likely to offer such a close view of so many manatees in such clear water. A boardwalk borders the entire spring run, with overlooks at several spots. Bring binoculars and use a camera lens with a polarizer for the best view of Florida's mermaids.

The boardwalk and Nature Trail at Blue Spring State Park near Orlando offer excellent close-up views of manatees in the clear spring run during the winter months.

Start: Parking lot bordering the St. Johns River

Distance: 1.0-mile out-and-back boardwalk hike

Difficulty: Easy, also wheelchair accessible

Hiking time: 30–60 minutes, depending on how many manatees are present and how much the animals interest you

Seasons: Dec to early Mar, depending on how long low temperatures remain. It must be below 68°F for manatees to remain in the spring run

Fees and permits: Admission fee of $6 per vehicle

Trail contact: Blue Spring State Park, 2100 W. French Ave., Orange City 32763; (386) 775-3663; floridastateparks.org/parks-and-trails/blue-spring-state-park

Schedule: 8:00 a.m. to sunset daily

Dog-friendly: Leashed pets permitted

Trail surface: Boardwalk and sand/dirt

Land status: Florida state park

Nearest town: Orange City

Other trail users: The general public, which is fascinated with manatees. School groups are sometimes brought here on weekdays.

Water availability: Restrooms, food concession

Maps: Available at the park

Overnight lodging: The park has 6 cabins, each with 2 bedrooms, heat, air-conditioning, and a full kitchen. No pets are allowed in the cabins. The park also has 51 developed campsites. More information at (800) 326-3521 and reserve.floridastateparks.org/Web/#!park/9.

Amenities: The following are available only after the manatees leave the spring run: boat tours, fishing, paddling, scuba diving, snorkeling, swimming, and tubing. Camping and picnicking are possible year-round.

Cell service: Good

Trail conditions: Rain may make the boardwalk slippery. The terrain is flat, so this is an easy walk. The trail is usually accessible for wheelchairs. Double-check conditions with a ranger before visiting.

12 Blue Spring Boardwalk and Nature Trail

Distance: 1 mile out and back

Finding the trailhead: *From the east coast* or I-95 on I-4 between Daytona and Orlando, take exit 114 and follow the Blue Spring State Park signs. Go south on US 17/92 to Orange City for about 2.5 miles. Turn right onto West French Avenue, which leads to the park entrance on the left. Drive to the main parking lot, which overlooks the St. Johns River. The boardwalk borders the river.

From Orlando, on I-4 take exit 111B toward Orange City. Go 0.4 mile and turn right onto Enterprise Road. Drive for 0.9 mile and turn right onto South Volusia Avenue, which turns into North Volusia Avenue in 1.7 miles. Proceed straight on North Volusia for another 0.2 mile, then turn left onto West French Avenue, which leads to the park entrance on the left. Drive to the main parking lot, which overlooks the St. Johns River. The boardwalk borders the river. Trailhead GPS: 28.952200 / -81.333541

The Hike

This 0.5-mile-long walk borders the edges of the clear spring run, which is connected to the St. Johns River. Wheelchair accessible, the boardwalk has several platforms overlooking the water to provide excellent views of the manatees. As they

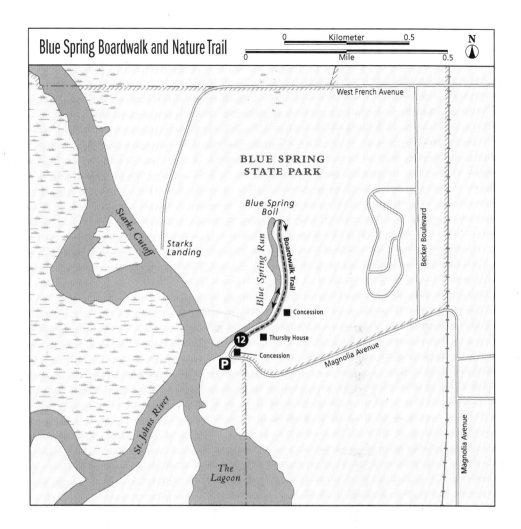

Kilometer 0.5

Mile 0.5

N

BLUE SPRING
STATE PARK

Blue Spring
Boil

Starks Cutoff

Starks
Landing

Blue Spring Run

Boardwalk Trail

Becker Boulevard

West French Avenue

■ Concession

12

■ Thursby House

P

Concession

Magnolia Avenue

St. Johns River

Magnolia Avenue

*The
Lagoon*

rest in the constant 72°F spring run, the best way to view the animals is with polarized sunglasses that reduce reflected glare on the water. As mammals, manatees are susceptible to cold and need to spend winters in refuges like this one. Once the St. Johns River warms up, the manatee herd disperses until the following November or December. No vegetation grows in the spring run, so manatees have to make frequent short forays into the cold St. Johns River for food each winter.

The best time to view the full herd of manatees is early in the morning when the park opens and temperatures are in the 50s or low 60s. There may be several hundred animals resting on the bottom of the spring run. Each one will rise occasionally to the surface to loudly inhale a breath of fresh air. It is an unforgettable sight.

Visit on a weekday to avoid crowds. Manatees are an extremely popular attraction, and the park often fills on winter weekends. Cars line up and wait for parking spaces to empty. Even weekdays can be crowded, with occasional busloads of schoolchildren, but they typically do not arrive before 10 a.m.

Beyond the area where manatees stay, the boardwalk enters a heavily wooded hammock and stops at the boil of Blue Spring. The water pressure there is strong enough to cause turbulent bubbling or upwelling in the spring pool. Fish life in the immediate vicinity of the boil is scarce due to the water's low oxygen content. However, fish become quite abundant just a few hundred feet down the run—particularly garfish and big tilapia.

When retracing your steps to the trailhead, don't overlook the large white house on the left. The Thursby House, one of the original plantation houses on the St. Johns, dates from 1872.

Miles and Directions

0.0　Start from the parking lot closest to the St. Johns River. Go straight toward the river and turn right to join the boardwalk bordering the spring.

0.2　Overlook of the spring run. Concessions and manatee presentations are in the small complex of buildings behind the boardwalk.

0.5　Arrive at an overlook of Blue Spring Boil. It is possible to swim/dive here when manatees are not present.

1.0　Arrive back at the parking lot.

Geneva Wilderness Area

Located in Seminole County between the towns of Oviedo and Geneva, the 180-acre Geneva Wilderness Area offers a good variety of scenery. Its native plant communities range from mixed hardwood swamp and mesic hammocks (sort of in between a dry and a wet hammock) to low-growing oaks in areas of bare white sand. Animals you might see include gopher tortoises, white-tailed deer, wild turkeys, sandhill cranes, and songbirds.

For a walk longer than the 1.7-mile main loop, take the blue-blazed Flagler Trail from the Geneva Wilderness Area to connect with the Little Big Econ State Forest. It takes about 3 hours to make the Little Big Econ circuit from the Geneva Wilderness Area trailhead. It's not a trek many make, since there are shorter routes to the state forest and the Econ River.

Start: Just off SR 426, south of the town of Geneva

Distance: 1.7-mile loop, with the option to add more miles

Difficulty: Easy to moderate, depending on wetness

Hiking time: 40 minutes to 3 hours, depending on the route you choose

Seasons: mid-Nov to mid-May

Fees and permits: None required

Trail contact: Seminole County Natural Lands Planning & Development; (407) 665-2001; seminolecountyfl.gov/departments-services/ leisure-services/parks-trails-and-natural-lands/

Schedule: Open daylight hours. Ed Yarborough Nature Center is open the first Sat of the month from 9 a.m. to noon; (407) 665-7432. Seminole County Natural Lands contacts are available weekdays from 8 a.m. to 5 p.m.

Dog-friendly: Leashed dogs permitted

Trail surface: Natural surface, bridges and boardwalks

Land status: Seminole County Natural Land (preserve)

Nearest town: Geneva

Other trail users: Cyclists possible in some sections but usually only hikers

Water availability: At the restroom but best to bring your own

Maps: Available online at seminolecountyfl .gov/core/fileparse.php/34/urlt/GWA-Trail -Guide-NEW-BW.pdf

Amenities: Parking, restrooms at the Ed Yarborough Nature Center (3543 CR 426; 407-349-0769); also exhibits and displays about the area's ecology

Cell service: Good

Trail conditions: Depending on the weather, part of the trail may be wet or partially flooded. The flat path is an easy hike in the dry winter season. Pack insect repellent regardless of the time of year.

13 Geneva Wilderness Area Loop

Distance: 1.8-mile loop

Finding the trailhead: *From I-4,* exit to Longwood at SR 434 and go east for 13 miles to Oviedo. Turn left onto SR 426 and go west for about 6 miles. The Geneva Wilderness Area is located at 3485 CR 426.

From the Geneva Wilderness Area trailhead, you can hike the short Geneva Wilderness loop trail or join the Flagler Trail for a longer hike.

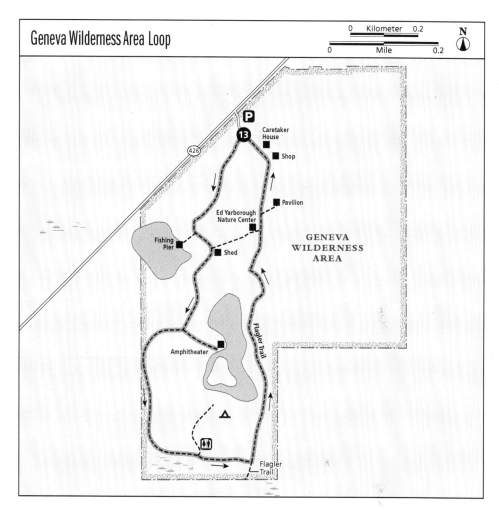

Geneva Wilderness Area Loop

0 Kilometer 0.2

0 Mile 0.2

N

P

13

Caretaker House

Shop

426

Pavilion

Ed Yarborough Nature Center

Fishing Pier

Shed

GENEVA WILDERNESS AREA

Amphitheater

Flagler Trail

Flagler Trail

From I-95, go west on SR 46 until you reach the town of Geneva (about 16 miles). Turn left and go south on CR 426 (Geneva Drive) for about 2 miles. The park entrance is on your left. Trailhead GPS: 28.708800 / -81.123967

The Hike

This hike may flood after heavy rains, and sections may be closed. Call (407) 665-2211 if you have any concerns or questions. Sign the register before beginning the hike. Two trails start from the information kiosk and run parallel for a time. The loop trail is blazed in red and takes 45 to 60 minutes to complete. The second trail, with yellow blazes, continues south to join the Flagler Trail that leads to Little Big Econ State Forest.

This description is of the loop trail only, which has a 0.3-mile access trail that ends at a clearing, the official start of the hike. Follow the red blazes as they point toward a pond. The trail arrives at a shallow pond that sometimes affords good wildlife viewing in dry weather. The pond has never completely dried up, but it sometimes comes close. It refills when the rains return and the water table rises.

At the pond, walk out on the dock for the chance to see wildlife on both the lake and the shoreline. After walking back to land, examine the shoreline more closely to find small plants that look like strawberry or orange jam. Those are clusters of tiny sundews, insectivorous wildflowers helping to control the local mosquito population. Sundews are usually are found with other carnivorous plants, such as pitcher plants and bladderworts.

Although none of its residents claim Swiss heritage, the ancestry of Geneva residents is amazingly diverse: 10.96 percent German, 17.1 percent English, 15.51 percent Irish, 10.35 percent French, 9 percent American, 4.32 percent Scottish, and 7.17 percent Italian.

From the dock, the trail continues along the pond shore then turns to go south. Keep an eye out for fire ants, which have been encountered near the trail. In a short time, a spur trail to the left leads to an amphitheater. Continue straight to follow the main path.

The trail turns left and goes around a pond you may not be able to see through the trees. The hike passes a turnoff on the left that leads to South Camp, a group campsite shaded by large oaks. When conditions are not overly dry, the camp is provided with campfire wood. The trail soon intersects the yellow diamond–blazed Flagler Trail that leads south to the Little Big Econ State Forest. The Geneva Trail turns left to return to the trailhead.

On the return, the trail parallels a pond before eventually arriving at restrooms that mark both the end and start of the loop trail. Continue straight and return to the parking lot for a total of 1.8 miles.

As for the Flagler Trail, how much more do you want to hike? It continues south for about 1.4 miles to enter the Little Big Econ State Forest, where the yellow blazes change to blue rectangles. This walk extends the hike by an additional 2.8 miles.

Miles and Directions

0.0 Start from information kiosk and approach the junction of the Flagler Trail (yellow diamond blazes) and the featured Geneva Wilderness loop trail (red diamond blazes). Follow the red-blazed loop trail.

0.3 Arrive at the restrooms. The loop trail officially starts here. From the trailhead, the red diamond blazes soon parallel a pond shoreline. The trail then arrives at a pier.

0.5 After leaving the pond, the trail goes south between two lakes and then bears left.

0.7 Pass the junction with a primitive group camping area. The Geneva Wilderness loop turns left (north) to return to the restrooms and the parking lot.

0.8 Go left on the Geneva Wilderness Trail to return to the parking lot.

1.4 Remaining on the loop trail, you pass a trail to the Ed Yarborough Nature Center and restroom area. Continue straight to return to the trailhead and the parking lot.

1.7 Arrive back at the parking lot.

Tibet-Butler Preserve

Anyone visiting the nearby theme parks should spend several (fee-free!) hours walking these self-guided interpretive nature trails and also view the exhibits at its educational environmental center. The Tibet-Butler Preserve is a rare chance to see real nature in the midst of the world's theme park capital. Did we mention it was fee-free? This is of the few places in the area that is.

Virtually surrounded by huge theme parks and housing developments, the 438-acre Tibet-Butler Preserve is one of the few natural areas remaining on the west side of Orlando. The preserve is located on the northeast side of Lake Tibet-Butler, part of the Butler Chain of Lakes.

In addition to several miles of hiking trails, the park also contains the Vera Carter Environmental Center, with an excellent interpretation program about the plants and animals found on the preserve.

Start: Behind the Vera Carter Environmental Center

Distance: Series of short trails that total about 4 miles; most trails are under 1 mile.

Difficulty: Easy except for the Palmetto Trail. During the rainy season, contact the preserve about trail conditions: (407) 254-1940.

Hiking time: A leisurely 1.5-2 hours

Seasons: Nov to May

Fees and permits: None required

Trail contact: Tibet-Butler Preserve, 8777 CR 535, Orlando 32836; (407) 254-1940; orangecountyfl.net/cultureparks/parks .aspx?m=dtlvw&d=39#.ZF_9AnbMLSw

Schedule: Open 8 a.m. to 6 p.m. daily; office closed Sun

Dog-friendly: Only service animals permitted

Trail surface: Mix of natural and paved trails

Land status: Orange County park

Nearest town: Windermere

Other trail users: None; paths are for walking only.

Water availability: Visitor center might have some but best to bring your own

Maps: Available at the environmental center

Amenities: The environmental center has air-conditioning, restrooms, rocking chairs, and a water bottle refilling station. Don't overlook the butterfly garden, which sometimes is full of living colors.

Cell service: Good

Trail conditions: Depending on the weather, some trails may be wet or partially flooded. Wear suitable footwear. The Palmetto Trail is not recommended for young children due to its frequently wet condition. It also has uneven ground and troublesome exposed tree roots. Other trails here consist of grassy paths and boardwalks. The preserve is not a well-shaded area, so come prepared for sun. Those in wheelchairs have only limited access. Insect repellent could be needed.

The great egret is a tall wading bird over 4 feet in height, with a wingspan of more than 50 inches.

14 Circuit of Nature Trails

Distance: 4.0 miles round-trip

Finding the trailhead: From I-4, take exit 68 at Lake Buena Vista and go north past the shopping centers onto CR 535 (also Winter Garden–Vineland Road). The preserve is 5 miles ahead, on the right. Trailhead GPS: 28.440974 / -81.541779

The Hike

These trails include uplands and wetlands, with a trail guide available inside the environmental center. To start your hike, turn right behind the center to join the self-guided 0.86-mile Pine Circle Interpretive Trail. The walk follows an old fire plowline used to fight a wildfire here in the late 1980s. The trail goes through pine flatwoods

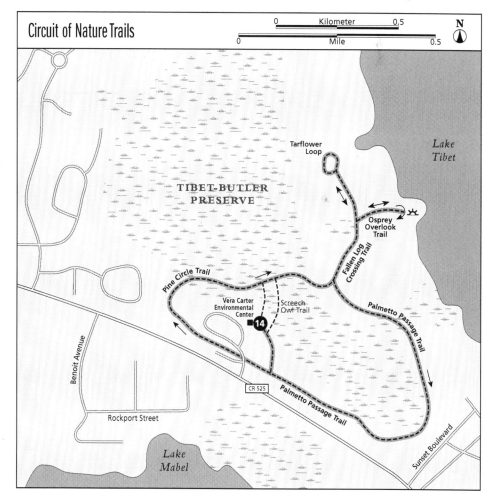

Circuit of Nature Trails

and oak hammocks, past longleaf pine and saw palmetto. Look for gopher tortoises in the native plants garden. The bobcats and foxes living here are very elusive.

The Pine Circle Interpretive Trail joins the 0.54-mile Fallen Log Crossing Trail, a boardwalk that penetrates deeper into a swampy area containing both cypress and pine trees. Fallen Log Crossing Trail ends when it intersects the 0.13-mile Osprey Overlook and the 0.49-mile Tarflower Loop Trails.

The Osprey Overlook Trail leads to a marsh adjacent to Lake Tibet-Butler. It's a very scenic area, with lots of lily pads and cypress trees decorated with long white beards of Spanish moss. This area is particularly good for bird-watching.

Leaving the Osprey Overlook Trail, turn right to join the 0.5-mile Tarflower Loop you passed earlier. If on other hikes you noticed a woody evergreen shrub with striking white to pinkish flowers with dark black seeds, you may have been looking at a tarflower but not known what it was. You'll see plenty of them here on the Tarflower Loop. Hike straight ahead on the soft white sand trail. Turn left after reaching a bench and walk through a scrub forest of woody shrubs and small trees. This is the place to find the tarflower bushes.

From the Tarflower Loop, retrace your steps a short distance to rejoin the Fallen Log Crossing Trail. You'll soon join the 1.08-mile Palmetto Passage, which follows a significant stretch of the preserve's perimeter. This is not only the park's longest but also its most difficult hike. Palmettos are notorious for having thick roots that grow near the surface. The roots are easy to stumble over if you don't pay attention to where your feet go. Palmetto Passage is not recommended for young children and anyone with balance problems.

The thick foliage along Palmetto Passage stays wet for a considerable time after it rains. Follow Palmetto Passage until it turns right onto the Pine Circle Trail. You're now returning to the environmental center and the end of the hike.

Miles and Directions

0.0   Start behind the Vera Carter Environmental Center; turn right to reach the Pine Circle Trail.

0.2   Reach the Pine Circle Trail; go right.

0.8   Come to a junction with the Fallen Log Crossing Trail; turn left to join Fallen Log Crossing. (*Option:* Turn right to return to the environmental center.)

1.2   A junction with the Palmetto Passage Trail comes in from the right. Continue straight on the Fallen Log Crossing Trail.

1.5   Fallen Log Crossing ends at the Osprey Overlook Trail, which takes you to the observation platform on Lake Tibet. Afterward, retrace your steps to the junction with the Fallen Log Crossing Trail; go right and join the Tarflower Loop.

2.2   The Tarflower Loop ends. Retrace your steps and go straight to rejoin Fallen Log Crossing.

2.6   Turn left to take the Palmetto Passage, a partial perimeter trail.

3.8   Turn right onto the Pine Circle Trail.

4.0   The circuit hike ends at the Vera Carter Environmental Center. (*Option:* One trail you haven't hiked is the Screech Owl Trail, a very short loop beside the environmental center.)

Withlacoochee State Forest

A snowy egret elegantly picks its way along a lake edge. These birds were once slaughtered for their plumes.

Divided into eight tracts, Withlacoochee State Forest is Florida's third-largest state forest. It comprises 157,479 acres and spans five counties: Citrus, Pasco, Lake, Hernando, and Sumter. It takes its name from the winding Withlacoochee River ("Little Big Water"), which flows for 13 miles through the forest. The World Wildlife Fund has called this forest area "One of the 10 Coolest Places in North America You've Never Seen." However, several million people do visit annually, especially from March to November, when the landscape usually is filled with brilliantly colored wildflowers.

The following hike description covers one of the forest's most popular short walks, the McKethan Lake Nature Trail Loop, a 1.9-mile loop with numerous interpretive signs. This is also referred to as the McKethan Lake Day-Use Area.

Start: Kiosk at the McKethan Lake parking area

Distance: 1.9 miles

Difficulty: Easy

Hiking time: 1–1.5 hours; this is a leisurely walk.

Seasons: Mid-Nov to May

Fees and permits: Daily user fee of $2 must be paid online in advance of visit. Annual pass available for $45, good for up to six people at a time. To purchase a day pass or make a camping reservation, visit reserveamerica.com or call (877) 879-3859.

Trail contact: Withlacoochee State Forest Visitor Center, 15003 Broad St., Brooksville 34601; (352) 797-4140; fdacs.gov/Forest-Wildfire/Our-Forests/State-Forests/Withlacoochee-State-Forest

Schedule: Forest access is from sunrise until sundown. The visitor center is located on US 41 about 7 miles north of Brooksville. Open weekdays from 8 a.m. to noon and 1 to 4 p.m. Closed weekends. Hours may change at any time.

Dog-friendly: No pets allowed

Trail surface: Mixed natural and man-made materials

Land status: Florida state forest

Nearest town: Brooksville

Other trail users: None; no bikes or horses allowed

Water availability: Bring your own

Maps: Available from the forestry visitor center and online

Amenities: Picnic tables, grills, restrooms, and a playground; fishing allowed with the proper license

Cell service: Good

Trail conditions: This should be flat, easy walking. Take bug repellent, just in case. The trail crosses a paved road several times. Walk against the traffic.

15 McKethan Lake Nature Trail Loop

Distance: 1.9-mile loop

Finding the trailhead: From US 41 in Brooksville, go north 7 miles; turn left at the McKethan Lake Day-Use Area sign. The entrance road is the second paved road north of the intersection of US 41 and Lake Lindsay Road (CR 476). The trailhead is on the right, at the end of the paved one-way road that circles the lake. The address is 15185 Broad St., Brooksville.

In Inverness, from the intersection of SR 44 and US 41, go south on US 41 for 12 miles. Turn right at the McKethan Lake Day-Use Area sign. The entrance road is the second paved road north of the intersection of US 41 and Lake Lindsay Road (CR 476). The trailhead is on the right, at the end of the paved one-way road that circles the lake. Trailhead GPS: 28.643591 / -82.335058

The Hike

The McKethan Lake Nature Trail Loop is a 1.9-mile loop hike through an unusually diverse forest system. Remarkably, all four species of southern pine (loblolly, sand, slash, and longleaf) grow along the trail. Wildlife includes armadillos (which dig triangular-shaped holes along the trail), opossums, raccoons, bobcats, foxes, white-tailed deer, and gray squirrels. Gopher tortoises and golden silk spiders are also quite common.

McKethan Lake is a bird sanctuary, home to scores of birds and part of the Great Florida Birding and Wildlife Trail. This is why dogs are not welcome here.

Native birds you might see include mottled ducks, anhingas, tricolored herons, snowy egrets, white and glossy ibises, and possibly wood storks. Visiting migratory birds include purple martins, chimney swifts, sedge wrens, swamp sparrows, and summer tanagers.

On this easy hike, keep an eye out for elm trees with parallel rows of holes. Those holes are made by the yellow-bellied sapsucker, which migrates to Florida in the winter. It pecks just deep enough to access the nutritious sap from the inner bark.

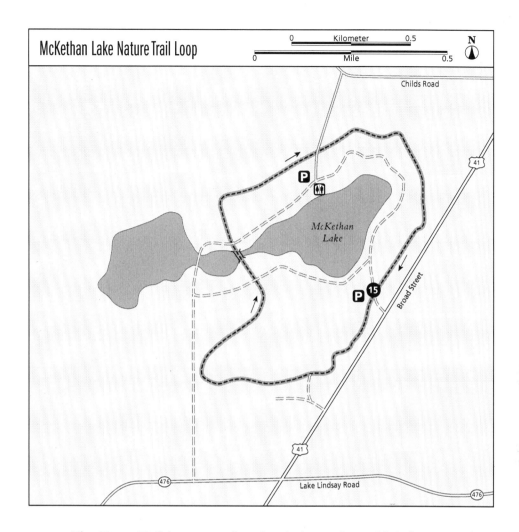

McKethan Lake Nature Trail Loop

The Nature Trail has twenty-four descriptive markers with information about forestry ecology. Highlighted plants and trees include devil's-walking-stick, a small tree whose trunk is covered with prickly spines; tree sparkleberry, an understory plant with leathery oval leaves and bark suitable for tanning leather; and resurrection fern, which alternates from bright green when moisture is plentiful to a drab brown during drought.

Marker 12 displays the poison ivy plant, something well worth remembering. If you are unfamiliar with the plant, take a picture and never go near it. It is the number one plant in Central Florida to avoid. One of the most colorful shrubs is the American beautyberry, which fills with reddish-purple berries from August to September. The berries are a favorite of deer, quail, and other wildlife.

Miles and Directions

0.0 Start at the trailhead, near the entrance of the parking lot. Walk the trail clockwise to follow the numbered markers in sequence.

0.2 Enter bottomland hardwood forest; go straight.

0.7 A footbridge crosses McKethan Lake. The trail goes right and returns to the forest.

1.2 Pass an American holly hammock and arrive at the picnic and restroom area.

1.6 Encounter a stand of longleaf pine; continue straight.

1.9 Arrive back at the parking lot.

Day Hikes

Bulow Plantation Ruins Historic State Park and Bulow Creek State Park

The Bulow Woods Trail is a striking 6.8-mile section of the Florida National Scenic Trail (FNST) connecting Bulow Plantation Ruins Historic State Park with Bulow Creek State Park. The hike features the ruins of Florida's largest east coast sugar mill (destroyed in 1836 during the Second Seminole War) and the magnificent Fairchild Oak, one of the largest live oak trees in the South, estimated to be 400 to 500 years old.

Start: Trailhead at a large sign just before the Bulow Plantation park gate. *Note:* Once your vehicle is past the gate, you must pay the day-use fee. Pull-offs are available outside the gate.

Distance: 6.8 miles one-way if you have a shuttle or 13.6 miles out and back (from Bulow Plantation); loop of varying lengths depending on starting point

Difficulty: Moderate. Best done in the dry winter months. The rainy season is likely to create sections of shallow standing water, making the trail very muddy in places. Mosquitoes can be annoying. These factors push the hike outside the "Easy" category.

Hiking time: 5–6 hours for the out-and-back; time for loop depends on starting point

Seasons: Nov to May for the best weather

Fees and permits: $4 to park your vehicle inside the Bulow Plantation gate; no fee to park outside the gate

Trail contact: Bulow Creek State Park, 3351 Old Dixie Hwy., Ormond Beach 32174; (386) 676-4050; floridastateparks.org/parks-and -trails/bulow-creek-state-park (phone number connects with Tomoka State Park, located several miles south)

Schedule: Trail open for day use from 8:30 a.m. to sunset year-round

Dog-friendly: Leashed dogs permitted

Trail surface: Dirt and sand path, boardwalks, some paved areas

Land status: Florida state park

Nearest town: Ormond Beach

Other trail users: Mountain bikers, nature lovers

Water availability: Bring your own

Maps: Available at nearby Tomoka State Park (386-676-4050), 4.5 miles south of Bulow Creek State Park on Old Dixie Highway, or from the Florida Trail Association (FTA)

Special considerations: Accessible restrooms and a picnic pavilion are available. Service animals are welcome.

Amenities: Bicycling, camping, fishing, geocaching, paddling, and picnicking. Many of these activities are actually available at nearby Tomoka State Park and not at the Bulow Ruins or Bulow Creek.

Cell service: Good

Trail conditions: This hike may require wading in the rainy season. Call ahead for current trail conditions. Have bug repellent with you regardless of the time of year. There are more than half a dozen boardwalks along this trail.

16 Bulow Woods Linear Trail

Distance: 6.8 miles one way

Finding the trailhead: Take exit 268 off I-95 and travel east less than a mile on Old Dixie Highway to CR 2001 (Old Kings Road), on the left. Go north 2 miles to the brown-and-white state marker at Plantation Road, called Monument Road on some maps. Turn right into Bulow Plantation Ruins Historic State Park. Parking for the hike is on the entrance road before the gate. Trailhead GPS: 29.434253 / -81.138069

The Hike

The Florida Trail Association refers to this trail as the Bulow Creek Trail. This guide uses "Bulow Woods Trail," since that's the name used by the two state parks sharing the hike.

Start the linear hike from the trailhead just outside the gate at Bulow Plantation Ruins Historic State Park. The Bulow Woods Trail crosses open woods and uses a series of footbridges before entering Bulow Hammock. The forest there is home to deer, foxes, bobcats, and a variety of birds, including pileated woodpeckers and bald eagles.

The trail passes stands of big live oaks that shade a good part of the Bulow Woods hike, not something that happens often enough in Central Florida.

At about the hike's midpoint, intersect a blue-blazed side trail to what is jokingly called the Cisco Rapids. The Cisco Ditch resembles a small waterfall and won't impress some people, but in Florida any waterfall is a rare sight.

The linear trail bypasses the 2.2-mile Bulow Woods Loop Trail. After moving through some marvelous old forest as well as a corridor of royal palms, the trail crosses a salt marsh at scenic Cedar Creek. The hike ends at the sprawling Fairchild Oak, Florida's most ancient oak tree. Some have estimated its age at an incredible 2,000 years. State botanists say the tree is actually between 400 and 500 years old.

The immense 68-foot-tall tree has a girth of about 24 feet. The tree's huge crown gives it a strong presence. The thick gnarled branches spread out almost as wide as the tree is tall and point to the sky in all directions. The Fairchild Oak looks bigger than life, like something cobbled together by a special effects team for *The Hobbit* or *Lord of the Rings*.

The name "Fairchild Oak" commemorates the invaluable work of David Fairchild, a plant explorer and botanist who worked for the US Department of Agriculture and journeyed around the world. During his travels he sent back seeds or cuttings of more than 200,000 species of fruits, vegetables, and grains. His department, the Office of Foreign Seed and Plant Introduction, researched and distributed some of the newfound crops to farmers around the country. Fairchild's influence on American cuisine cannot be overstated. He helped introduce soybeans, pistachios, mangoes, nectarines, dates, and flowering cherry trees.

The Bulow Woods Trail ends near the magnificent Fairchild Oak, an estimated 400 to 500 years old.

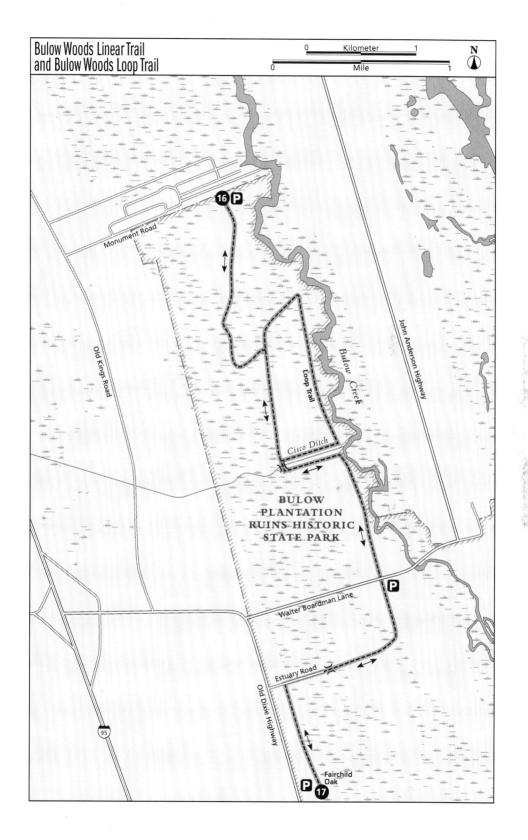

Kilometer
0   1

Mile
0   1

N

Monument Road

Old Kings Road

John Anderson Highway

16 P

Loop Trail

Bulow Creek

Cisco Ditch

BULOW
PLANTATION
RUINS HISTORIC
STATE PARK

P

Walter Boardman Lane

Estuary Road

Old Dixie Highway

95

P

Fairchild
Oak

17

Bulow Woods Trail sign

Miles and Directions

0.0 Start at the marked trailhead, just before the front gate of Bulow Plantation Ruins Historic State Park.

0.2 Cross a stream on a footbridge.

0.7 Cross a second footbridge.

1.2 Cross yet another footbridge.

1.4 Reach a wetter area requiring two footbridges to cross.

1.6 Pass a junction with the green-blazed Bulow Woods Loop Trail.

2.0 Reach Marsh Point.

2.8 The trail follows the Cisco Ditch, a canal that is part natural and part man-made.

3.2 Pass the blue-blazed side trail to "Cisco Rapids." (**Option:** Go view the curiosity.)

3.8 Cross a power line right-of-way.

4.9 Cross the paved Walter Boardman Lane.

5.5 Cross Cedar Creek on a footbridge.

6.8 Arrive at the Fairchild Oak, located at the parking area in Bulow Creek State Park. Unless you've arranged for a shuttle or a pickup, prepare to retrace your steps.

17 Bulow Woods Loop Trail

Distance: Depends on starting point

From Bulow Plantation Ruins Historic State Park

Finding the trailhead: Take exit 268 off I-95 and travel east less than a mile on Old Dixie Highway to CR 2001 (Old Kings Road), on the left. Go north 2 miles to the brown-and-white state marker at Plantation Road, called Monument Road on some maps. Turn right into Bulow Plantation Ruins Historic State Park. Parking for the hike is on the entrance road before the gate. Trailhead GPS: 29.434253 / -81.138069

The Hike

Follow the Bulow Woods Trail until it reaches a junction at 1.5 miles. There you have the option of visiting the Cisco Ditch by either the Palm Hammock Loop Trail or the Marsh Trail. To hike the Bulow Woods Loop, go straight on the green-blazed Marsh Trail. The trail enters a hammock of oaks and cabbage palms then passes a floodplain.

The elevation increases slightly before, at about 3.0 miles, you arrive at the fast-flowing Cisco Ditch. At that point transfer to the Pine Hammock Trail to begin hiking some of the best parts of the forest. A woodland tunnel takes you past very old and very tall oaks and pines. Trees of such size must be many hundreds of years old. They are a powerful remnant of the genuine old Florida, possibly predating the arrival of the Seminoles to Florida.

In another 0.7 mile, return to the beginning of the loop trail. Now retrace your steps back to the Plantation Ruins trailhead. Arriving there, you will have completed a hike of 5.2 miles.

From Bulow Creek State Park

Finding the trailhead: From Bulow Creek State Park, there are two starting points. The longest trail begins at the Fairchild Oak, the traditional trailhead for most Bulow Creek State Park hikes. You can also begin at the Walter Boardman Lane trailhead, which places you 1.9 miles closer to the Bulow Woods Loop Trail. The option you choose depends on how much you want to walk. The "Miles and Directions" below apply to both the long and short trails sections.

From the Fairchild Oak at Bulow Creek State Park: Hike an unusually straight path for the first 0.6 mile. Then turn right into an area that could be muddy in the rainy season. Palm trees border the path before the trail opens up when it enters a surprisingly scenic marshy area. At 1.3 miles cross Cedar Creek on a footbridge. The trail reaches a gate and turns left at 1.45 miles. Follow a forest road north. The trail crosses Walter Boardman Lane at 1.9 miles. There is a parking lot for starting the hike from here.

From Walter Boardman Lane: The hike from Walter Boardman Lane is about 4 miles shorter than from the Fairchild Oak. The Boardman trailhead places you 1.9 miles north of the Fairchild Oak. The return hike finishes at mile 7.0, for a total of 5.1 miles.

Miles and Directions

0.0 Start from the Fairchild Oak.

0.6 The trail makes a sharp turn right.

1.3 Cross Cedar Creek on a footbridge.

1.45 The trail turns left to head north.

1.9 Cross the Walter Boardman Lane parking lot.

2.15 Pass a side trail on the left leading to Boardman Pond.

2.30 The spur trail on the left leads to the Boardman Pond observation platform.

3.10 The trail turns left and changes to a different forest road.

3.25 The trail crosses the Cisco Canal on a footbridge.

3.4 Junction with the green-blazed Bulow Woods Loop Trail.

5.4 Complete the loop.

5.55 Rejoin the Florida Trail, going south.

7.0 Return to Walter Boardman Lane.

7.6 Recross Cedar Creek on a footbridge.

8.9 Arrive back at the Fairchild Oak in Bulow Creek State Park.

More Information

The 0.3-mile **Wahlin Trail**, located behind the Fairchild Oak in Bulow Creek State Park, leads to a location where fresh water flows out of the ground and under a bridge. One day, after eroding away enough limestone, this seepage stream could possibly become a freshwater spring.

Merritt Island National Wildlife Refuge

An alligator is just starting a stroll. It will lift its belly and tail to "high walk" and move faster.

The 140,000-acre Merritt Island Refuge was created from excess National Aeronautics and Space Administration (NASA) land during the development of the US space exploration program. Merritt Island NWR is one of Central Florida's principal wildlife habitats.

Much of the 35-mile-long barrier island is a huge expanse of chest-high salt marsh grass dotted with small ponds and hammocks, as well as mosquito control dikes dating from the 1950s. Merritt Island NWR houses more than 1,500 species of plants and wildlife, including almost 400 different kinds of birds. Strategically located on a major bird migration corridor known as the Atlantic Flyway, the refuge hosts numerous migratory species, which winter there between November and March.

More than 500 species of wildlife live on the refuge, including 15 listed as federally threatened or endangered. In addition, the refuge contains several wading bird rookeries, 2,500 Florida scrub jays, 33 active or potentially active bald eagle nests, and numerous osprey nests. During the spring months, manatees often swim in the nearby Indian River.

Wood stork out for a walk on its very long legs

MIGRATING BIRDS

From early fall through winter, migrating waterfowl appear at Merritt Island NWR in truly staggering numbers. Almost 400 species of birds have been recorded, and a good winter bird count goes something like this: 50,000 to 70,000 ducks, 100,000 coots, 12,000 to 14,000 gulls and terns, 2,000 raptors, and enormous numbers of songbirds.

In addition to the huge waterfowl migration, spectacular migrations of passerine birds such as warblers occur in spring and fall. Eight species of herons and egrets are commonly in residence. Nesting populations of bald eagles, brown pelicans, mottled ducks, and wood storks are special attractions. Prime birding times are always early and late in the day. Binoculars and a powerful telephoto lens enhance the experience tremendously. The best months for observing birds are November to March.

Those seriously interested in birding should obtain a copy of the bird checklist available at the visitor center before starting out. From September to February, visitors may be surprised to hear the sounds of shotguns so close to the hikes and Wildlife Drive. Duck hunting has been an annual ritual here for generations. It is still sanctioned, but only on a controlled quota basis. Hunting is considered an important part of waterfowl management, so the area is as much a wildlife management area as a wildlife refuge.

The following descriptions cover the three best hikes on the refuge: the 4.8-mile Allan Cruickshank Memorial Loop Trail, the 1.9-mile Palm Hammock Loop Trail, and the adjacent 0.7-mile Oak Hammock Loop Trail. The Palm and Oak Hammock Trails suffered considerable storm damage in 2023 and are under restoration as this is written. Palm Hammock is currently open to 0.65 mile; previously it was 1.9 miles.

Start: The Cruickshank Trail starts at the Black Point Wildlife Drive, Stop 8; the Palm and Oak Hammock Trails start from a parking lot 1.2 miles past the visitor center.

Distance: Hikes range from 0.7 mile to 4.8 miles.

Difficulty: Easy to moderate, depending on how wet the ground is

Hiking time: About 3 hours for all three hikes

Seasons: Nov to May; migratory waterfowl are present in winter months.

Fees and permits: Daily pass of $10 per vehicle, $25 for annual pass. Daily pass for on foot/bicycle is $10. Passes can be purchased at the visitor center when open or online at recreation.gov/sitepass/1513. When the visitor center is closed, day passes are available at the entrance to the Black Point Wildlife Drive, located off Max Brewer Memorial Highway.

Trail contact: Merritt Island National Wildlife Refuge, 1963 Refuge Headquarters Rd., Titusville 32782; (321) 861-0667; fws.gov/refuge/merritt-island. The visitor information center is about 5 miles east of US 1, on SR 402.

Schedule: Hiking trails are open during daylight hours; the visitor information center is open Tues through Sat, 8 a.m. to 4 p.m.; closed Sun and Mon. Find the dates for waterfowl hunting season at fws.gov/merrittisland/waterfowlhunting/index.html.

Dog-friendly: No pets permitted
Trail surface: Natural path, boardwalk, and short footbridges
Land status: National wildlife refuge
Nearest town: Titusville
Other trail users: Birders
Water availability: The visitor center (when open); best to bring your own
Maps: Available at the visitor information center. Refuge trail maps are also available online at fws.gov/refuge/merritt-island/visit-us/trails.

Refuge overview map is available at www.nbbd.com/godo/minwr/pdf/MINWRmap00.pdf.
Special considerations: Migratory bird hunting takes place on certain days from Sept to mid-Feb. For information go to myfwc.com/license/limited-entry/merritt-island-waterfowl/.
Trail conditions: Flooding from a hurricane in the summer of 2023 significantly flooded the 1.9-mile Palm Hammock Loop Trail. As this is written, the trail is closed until it dries out. Other trails are open. Insect repellent is more vital than ever here.

18 Allan Cruickshank Memorial Loop Trail

Distance: 4.8-mile loop

Finding the trailhead: From I-95 just north of Titusville, take exit 220 toward SR 46. Drive east for 0.3 mile and turn right onto SR 406 (Max Brewer Memorial Highway). Follow SR 406 to Black Point Wildlife Drive. Turn left onto Black Point Wildlife Drive and travel 3.4 miles to the parking lot at Stop 8. The Allan Cruickshank Memorial Loop Trail begins here. Trailhead GPS: 28.678303 / -80.771879

The Hike

This trail is named for wildlife photographer and naturalist Allan D. Cruickshank, who was instrumental in the establishment of the refuge. The best time for hiking through what is considered one of Florida's premier birding areas is in early morning or midafternoon, when the birds are usually most active. The best hiking is from November to March, when birds are plentiful and the weather at its coolest.

The observation platform and a photography blind seen from the Wildlife Drive parking lot make a good rest stop for your return if you walk the trail counterclockwise. Regardless of the time of year, bring water and bug repellent.

The trail starts on a dirt road that soon turns rougher. As the path borders open water and mangroves, search the mangrove roots for birds and possibly an alligator. With as many as eight species of herons and egrets usually in residence, you should definitely sight wading birds. Brown pelicans, mottled ducks, wood storks, and bald eagles are also common. An alligator is likely to be in any of the drainage ditches you pass.

As you move around a small lagoon and pass a bench, there's a possible glimpse of the giant white Vehicle Assembly Building. The trail then continues atop an impoundment with open water on both sides.

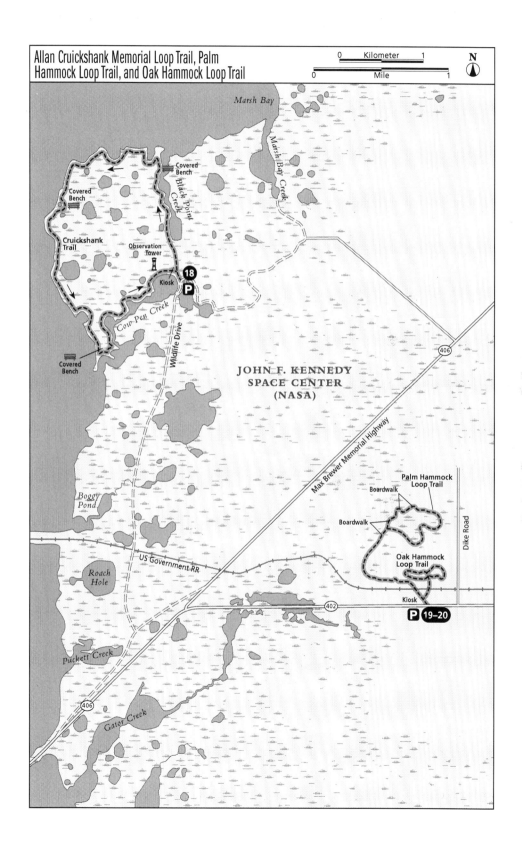

Allan Cruickshank Memorial Loop Trail, Palm Hammock Loop Trail, and Oak Hammock Loop Trail

Marsh Bay

Marsh Bay Creek

Covered Bench

Covered Bench

Black Point Creek

Cruickshank Trail

Observation Tower

Kiosk

18

P

Cow-Pen Creek

Covered Bench

Wildlife Drive

JOHN F. KENNEDY SPACE CENTER (NASA)

Max Brewer Memorial Highway

406

Boggy Pond

US Government RR

Roach Hole

406

Puckett Creek

Gator Creek

402

Palm Hammock Loop Trail

Boardwalk

Boardwalk

Oak Hammock Loop Trail

Dike Road

Kiosk

P 19–20

Kilometer
Mile

N

The pool of water on your right might appear to be a lake. It's actually Cow Pen Creek, coming off the Indian River. Once you arrive at the observation tower, it's only 0.02 mile back to the parking lot.

Miles and Directions

0.0 Start at the parking lot at Stop 8 on Black Point Wildlife Drive.

0.6 Pass the old boardwalk to a photographer's blind.

0.8 Pass a shaded bench.

1.4 Enjoy a panoramic view of the lagoon.

2.0 Reach Marker 3.

2.2 Pass a bench and a view of NASA's Vehicle Assembly Building, where spacecraft are prepped for flight.

3.0 Reach Marker 2.

3.7 Pass a covered bench.

4.6 Pass the observation tower.

4.8 Arrive back at the parking lot.

19 Palm Hammock Loop Trail

Distance: 1.9-mile lollipop loop

Finding the trailhead: From I-95 just north of Titusville, take exit 220 toward SR 46. Drive east for 0.3 mile and turn right onto SR 406 (Max Brewer Memorial Highway). Follow SR 406 for 2.8 miles. Then turn right onto SR 402 (Playalinda Beach Road). Go straight for 1.7 miles to reach the visitor information center. The common trailhead for the Palm and Oak Hammock Trails is I.2 miles on the left, beyond the visitor center. The two trails begin from a small parking lot. Each trailhead is clearly marked. Trailhead GPS: 28.644140 / -80.716606

The Hike

Both the Palm and Oak Hammock Trails áre home to songbirds, hawks, woodpeckers, owls, wrens, armadillos and more. Hammocks like these are common in areas between uplands and wetlands. Except during drought, they are naturally protected from fire due to the moisture permeating their landscapes.

The longer, 1.9-mile Palm Hammock Loop Trail is the tougher walk due to muddy and wet areas following rains. Several boardwalks span the wettest spots. You still should wear waterproof shoes or old sneakers, old socks, and long pants and a long-sleeved shirt to thwart mosquitoes. A sign at the trailhead may indicate whether to expect "wet," "dry," or "closed" conditions. In very wet periods, the trail may be rerouted, which the sign will indicate.

The Palm Hammock Loop Trail goes left from the common trailhead. Cross a short bridge and arrive at the NASA railroad tracks, actually a spur built from the Florida East Coast Railway. It transports 150-ton segments of NASA's solid rocket boosters. Using a small fleet of modified and specialized railroad cars has proven safer and less expensive than shipping rocket parts by cargo aircraft or barge.

After crossing the tracks, a boardwalk becomes the main trail and leads into a thick oak forest with tall saw palmettos. As this is written, the trail is undergoing restoration. Compare the map in this guide with the one posted online to see how much the trail might have changed.

Previously, the trail passed through cabbage palm hammocks, hardwood forest, and open marsh. Then, after passing through a sometimes-muddy area, the trail passed more large saw palmettos. After a right turn, the trail arrived at the start of the small loop trail through oaks and palms. After completing the loop, return to the main access trail to return to the parking lot.

Miles and Directions

0.0 Start from the parking lot on SR 402 and go left.

0.12 Cross the railroad tracks.

0.17 The trail veers to the left to enter a dense hammock.

0.66 Intersect the loop walk shortly after the trail turns right.

1.23 Complete the loop and start your return

1.90 Arrive back at the parking lot.

20 Oak Hammock Loop Trail

Distance: 0.7-mile loop

Finding the trailhead: This loop trail shares a common trailhead and parking lot with the Palm Hammock Loop Trail. Trailhead GPS: 28.644140 / -80.716606

The Hike

This 30-minute walk winds through a subtropical forest after you cross the NASA railroad tracks. The dense, bright green fern bed at the start of the hike is one of the more colorful parts of the plant community, as explained in a series of interpretive signs. In addition to walking in the shade of large live oak trees, you'll pass through a grove of citrus trees. Indian River oranges and grapefruit have been nationally famous, first planted in this area around 1830. This particular grove dates from the 1940s.

Miles and Directions

0.0 Start from the parking lot on SR 402, bearing right.

0.5 Turn left at the boardwalk.

0.7 Arrive back at the parking lot.

More Information

Visitor center boardwalk: Located behind the visitor center is a very good 0.5-mile trail on an accessible boardwalk that passes two freshwater ponds, a native butterfly garden, a hammock, and a wetland prairie. Interpretive signs and three benches are stationed along the boardwalk.

Manatee overlook: A manatee observation deck is located at Haulover Canal on the north side of the SR 3 bridge. The largest number of manatees usually appears in fall and spring.

De Leon Springs State Park

The gateway to the Wild Persimmon Trail is unusually elaborate for a state park.

The Mayaca Indians lived in this area for 6,000 years before the arrival of the Spanish. They called the freshwater spring here Acuera, or "Healing Waters." And although Juan Ponce de León probably never tested them, an 1889 advertisement promised visitors that the soda- and sulfur-impregnated waters would act as a veritable fountain of youth. If this were true, you'd see thousands of centenarians wandering around De Leon Springs, an area that has been occupied off and on for the past 8,000 years.

The spring has proven that it does have some magic. In 1985 it yielded two dugout canoes built 5,000 and 6,000 years ago, respectively. They are believed to be the oldest canoes ever discovered in the Western Hemisphere.

In the 1800s the park property was a cotton, corn, and sugar plantation called Spring Garden. Its sugar mill was powered by the current of the freshwater spring, which pours out 19 million gallons daily.

Tourism is to blame for the spring's current name. The Spring Garden area became a tourist destination when steamboats and the railroad began bringing people here. Like today, the local residents wanted to attract more tourists, so they changed the name from Spring Garden to Ponce de Leon Springs. Naturally, they said the spring waters were a "the Fountain of Youth."

Plan to visit on a weekday; avoid the weekends. The park is extremely popular due to the Old Sugar Mill Pancake House, open from 8 a.m. to 4 p.m. daily. When zealous pancake eaters fill the park to capacity, the gates close and open intermittently until traffic returns to normal in the afternoon. The main attraction of the pancake house is that you get to cook flapjacks at your table.

The 4.2-mile Wild Persimmon Trail was laid out and constructed by the Florida Trail Association. The hike loops through a scenic landscape of hammocks, floodplains, and fields.

Start: Parking lot behind the visitor center/ bath house area

Distance: 4.2-mile loop plus a 0.3-mile access trail (each way) on a paved access trail, for a hike of 4.8 miles

Difficulty: Easy, becoming moderate when sections flood during rainy periods. With high temperatures and humidity, summer hiking can be difficult.

Hiking time: 2–3 hours

Seasons: Best hiking during the cooler dry season, Dec to Apr

Fees and permits: Admission fee of $6 per vehicle. Hikers must sign in and obtain a map; they also must be back 1 hour before sunset.

Trail contact: De Leon Springs State Park, 601 Ponce de Leon Blvd., De Leon Springs 32130; (386) 985-4212; floridastateparks.org/deleon springs; pancake house: (386) 871-7573

Schedule: Open 8 a.m. to sundown daily

Dog-friendly: Leashed pets allowed on the trail but not in the swimming area

Trail surface: Paved road, boardwalks, bridges, natural surfaces, and some wet areas. Slippery-soled shoes or flip-flops make it easy to slip and fall.

Land status: Florida state park

Nearest town: DeLeon Springs

Other trail users: Nature lovers

Water availability: At the restroom or the restaurant. Bring your own liquid for the trail.

Maps: Consult the park's website; also ask for a brochure when you pay park admission.

Special considerations: Hikers must register at the ranger station before hitting the trail. An all-terrain and a standard wheelchair are available. Ask at the gate. A 0.5-mile wheelchair-accessible paved Nature Trail has interpretive signs.

Amenities: Visitor center, boat tours, restaurant, fishing, swimming, and snorkeling. No lifeguards or camping.

Cell service: Good

Trail conditions: This is a well-marked, well-maintained trail. About half the hike is along the edge of a swamp forest, which can sometimes be soggy. Come prepared with a good supply of insect repellent and shoes suitable for wet hiking. In rainy season, call the ranger station for a current trail update about whether the trail is open.

21 Wild Persimmon Trail

Distance: 4.8-mile lollipop

Finding the trailhead: From I-4, take exit 56 and follow SR 44 to DeLand. At DeLand, drive north on US 17 for approximately 6 miles, following the state park signs. Turn left onto Ponce de Leon Boulevard and go 1 mile to the park entrance. After paying the entrance fee, drive to the bottom of the hill. Ignore the paved nature trails. At the bottom of the hill, turn right and park behind the long building that has a bathhouse changing area and also serves as the park's visitor center. Trailhead GPS: 29.132622 / -81.360812

The Hike

There is no parking area at the trailhead, which is located 0.3 mile from the parking area. To reach the trailhead, you must hike a paved Nature Trail that was laid down when De Leon Springs was still a popular roadside attraction.

To access the trailhead, walk up the hill you just drove down until you reach a paved Nature Trail on the left. After just a short distance, you'll reach a side path/ boardwalk on the left to "Old Methuselah," a huge 150-foot-tall bald cypress estimated to be 500 years old. The walk to the tree is short, and the tree is worth seeing despite being partially obscured by an oak tree branch in front of the ancient cypress. The oak is overdue for a trim.

Continuing on the paved Nature Trail, painted red arrows point the way. From the Old Methuselah side trail, take a short hike until the paved trail turns left and goes up another hill. You can't miss the Wild Persimmon trailhead, on the right. It has what has to be Florida's fanciest trailhead markers: a giant cattle gate like you see in old Western movies or the TV show *Yellowstone*. A sign attached to gate's crossbeam makes it clear you've arrived at the Wild Persimmon Trail.

Another large ranch gate to the left of the Wild Persimmon Trail marks the start of the 0.5-mile Monkey Island Trail, which explores an area of thick ferns and dense palm hammocks. The trail also leads to the remnants of an old jungle cruise tour boat.

The Wild Persimmon Trail starts on a path that's deceivingly dry. After turning right, the trail enters a thick, junglelike setting—actually a floodplain where footbridges cross areas that are perpetually wet. Be sure you have insect repellent already applied to deter mosquitoes.

Sign for "Old Methuselah," an ancient cypress tree estimated to be 500 years old

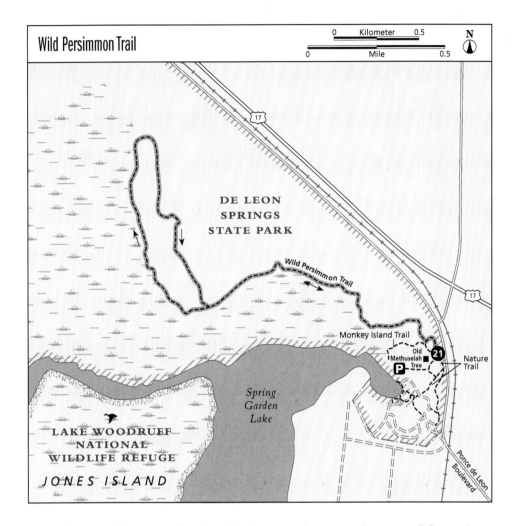

0   Kilometer   0.5

0   Mile   0.5

N

DE LEON
SPRINGS
STATE PARK

Wild Persimmon Trail

Monkey Island Trail

Old
Methuselah
Tree

21

Nature
Trail

P

Spring
Garden
Lake

LAKE WOODRUFF
NATIONAL
WILDLIFE REFUGE

JONES ISLAND

Ponce de Leon
Boulevard

Oak hammocks, a mix of hardwood and pine, and a cypress dome are all featured along this walk. Much of the hike goes through a hydric hammock—a forest of trees and plants that flourish in wet conditions. The park's forested areas are dominated by red maples, sweet gums, magnolias, cabbage palms, and water hickories.

The area here can be rich in wildlife, including deer, turkeys, Florida black bears, wild hogs, and fox squirrels. You should hear some distinctive sounds from songbirds and also the echoing noise of a woodpecker.

The trail also crosses an old shell mound left by the long-departed Mayaca, who once lived near the spring. The loop section begins at about 1.4 miles. The ground remains moist until you reach dry uplands where the persimmon trees are found, just beyond Marker 10. The persimmon tree, with oval-tipped leaves from 3 to 6 inches long, produces a small green fruit that becomes soft, sweet, and orange in color when it matures in the fall. It's a favorite of foxes, raccoons, and many bird species.

The remainder of the loop hike stays mostly on high ground. At 3.0 miles the loop closes and the trail returns to the floodplain forest. From there, retrace your steps to the parking lot.

Miles and Directions

0.0 Start from the parking lot behind the visitor center.

0.1 Pass a short boardwalk to Old Methuselah, an ancient cypress tree.

0.3 Begin the blue-blazed Wild Persimmon Trail.

0.5 Use a bridge to cross a stream.

0.8 Pass a bench. The trail may now become muddier, depending on rain.

0.9 The trail crosses the first in a series of four boardwalks.

1.0 Cross a stream; continue straight.

1.4 Go straight to join the loop and hike clockwise. Ignore the return path on the right.

1.8 Pass a second bench.

2.3 Reach the grove of persimmon trees in a meadow.

3.0 Complete the loop.

3.5 Pass a cypress dome.

4.5 Arrive back at the trailhead.

4.8 Arrive back at the parking area.

More Information

Swimming at De Leon Springs State Park is permitted from 8 a.m. until a half hour before sunset. The spring keeps the swimming area at a constant 72°F. Water depths range from 18 inches to maximum of 30 feet at the spring boil. Canoe rentals are available for exploring Spring Garden Creek, which provides access to the 22,000 acres of marshes, creeks, and lakes at the adjacent Lake Woodruff National Wildlife Refuge.

Black Bear Wilderness Area

The 1,600-acre Black Bear Wilderness Area (BBWA) is one of Central Florida's most popular hikes for seeing wildlife. It is located in an unlikely place: across from a major housing development. Big Bear Wilderness Area has many more surprises.

From the Black Bear parking lot, all you see is thick forest. There is no hint that almost 3 miles of the hike borders the St. Johns, Florida's longest river. Other parts of the trail are located within the St. Johns River floodplain, which contains wet prairie, hydric hammock, and cypress swamps. Most of the hiking trail is on high levees and boardwalks by the St. Johns River. However, there may be muddy sections on the loop hike. The out-and-back option ends before any muddy areas.

On this hike, you need to watch where you step. The dirt levees can be narrow, and in some places there are seemingly unending clusters of trippy, toe-stubbing tree roots. Black Bear is not a trail for young children or anyone with serious balance problems. A hiking stick would be handy and make the hike easier for anyone.

Although this hike is not listed with the "Overnight Hikes," the primitive campsite definitely is a site to consider.

Start: Just behind the kiosk in the parking lot

Distance: 7.1 miles for full loop trail; 2.0 miles for the out-and-back hike to the St. Johns River

Difficulty: Moderate to difficult in areas, with steep slopes, uneven ground, and a gauntlet of tree roots that grow across the path on both trails. Sections of the trail can be muddy and slick after rain.

Hiking time: 3-4 hours for the full loop; 1-1.5 hours for the out-and-back

Seasons: Mid-Nov to mid-May for the best hiking weather

Fees and permits: No fee; permit required to stay at the only primitive campsite. When camping, a copy of the permit must be displayed on the hiker's vehicle dashboard; camper must carry the original permit.

Trail contact: Seminole County Greenways and Natural Lands; (407) 665-2211; seminolecountyfl.gov/locations/black-bear-wilderness-area.stml

Schedule: The wilderness area is open dawn to dusk. The Natural Lands department is open 8 a.m. to 5 p.m. weekdays only. This WMA is an unmanned area with no visitor center or representative on site.

Dog-friendly: Leashed dogs allowed; owner must pick up and carry out animal waste.

Trail surface: Dirt, sand, and boardwalks

Land status: Seminole County Natural Land

Nearest town: Sanford

Other trail users: Hikers, birders, and nature lovers

Water availability: None except the St. Johns River; bring your own

Maps: Available online at seminolecountyfl .gov/locations/black-bear-wilderness-area.stml

Special considerations: Trail safety markers are placed every 0.5 mile. The trail is prone to flooding after heavy rains. The county does not offer any assurance that this Natural Land is safe for any purpose.

Camping: Black Bear has a primitive campsite that holds six people. It is a "pack in, pack out" camping area located about 3 miles from the trailhead. The site offers a fire ring and a small, covered pavilion. The nightly camping fee is $15. Register online at web1.myvscloud.com/wbwsc/flseminolectywt.wsc/.

A welcoming spot for a time-out on one of Central Florida's more challenging hikes

Amenities: Parking lot has a primitive toilet; no water available. This hike is not wheelchair accessible.

Cell service: Good

Trail conditions: Protruding tree roots in many sections require attention. Once the trail turns away from the St. Johns River to go inland, the walk becomes more challenging. The steep impoundment banks may require scrambling up and down. They can also be quite muddy. You wouldn't regret bringing a hiking pole.

22 Black Bear Wilderness Area Hike

Distance: 7.1 miles total

Finding the trailhead: Located at 5301 Michigan Ave., Sanford.

Going east on I-4, take the Sanford 17–72 exit. After the exit ramp finishes curving down, drive straight ahead to the stoplight at Orange Boulevard; turn right. Go 1.8 miles and turn right onto New York Street. Follow New York Street to where it meets Michigan Avenue. The Big Bear Wilderness Area parking lot is straight ahead.

Going West on I-4: Exit I-4 at SR 46 and go west. In a little over a mile, turn left onto Orange Boulevard. Go 1.8 miles and turn right onto New York Street. Follow New York Street to where it meets Michigan Avenue. The Big Bear Wilderness Area parking lot is straight ahead. Trailhead GPS: 28.832702 / -81.353830

The Hike

You have two hiking options. One is to hike the short original trail of only 1.0 mile that ends at the St. Johns River. If you decide you've seen enough forest, retrace your steps for an out-and-back hike of 2.0 miles. Expect the walk to be at a fairly leisurely pace due to the overabundance of tree roots.

Your second option is to walk the full 7.1-mile loop. The trail kiosk may have a map, although none is needed. The cell signal here is strong enough to follow your progress on Google Maps. Trail safety markers with GPS coordinates are usually placed every 0.5 mile. However, if you need to call for help, it could be a long time coming. There is no fast access to the trail.

The description begins with the out-and-back hike and then continues with the remainder of the full loop trail.

From the trailhead near the parking lot kiosk, follow the blue arrow markers to a wide paved path that enters a swamp. The pavement gives way to boardwalk at about 0.15 mile, where the trail splits to form a loop. Go right where the trail transfers to the top of a steep levee embankment lined with tree roots only partially buried in the ground. The trail has a nice mix of sun and shade, and songbirds and woodpeckers are common near the trailhead. Unusually scenic sections of junglelike paths make the rooty walk worthwhile. Keep an eye out for a Florida black bear as you hike. They frequent this area more than other locations, so the odds are in your favor.

The trail stays well above the canal and surrounding marshes and trees. You leave the canal at about 0.9 mile when the trail crosses a power line clearing and joins a boardwalk. The St. Johns River is just ahead.

The forest bordering the trail keeps river views limited. The out-and-back option officially ends at the 1.0 mile mark, but there's nothing to stop you from hiking more before turning back. For the next 3.0 miles, the boardwalk skirts the edge of the wilderness area as the trail travels northward along the St. Johns. Trees still obscure the river in some sections.

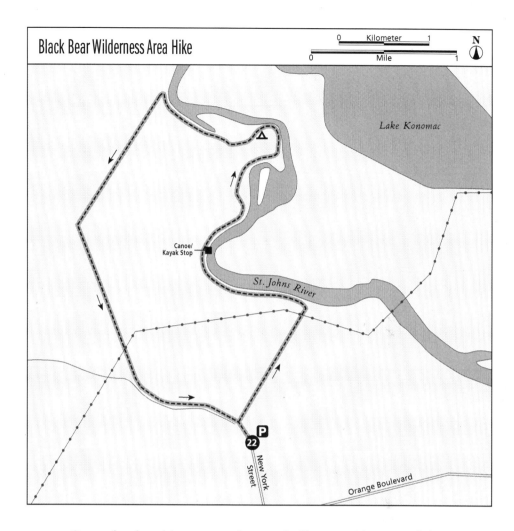

On weekends and in summer, the sound of boats cruising up and down the St. Johns always makes the river feel close. Florida's longest river, the St Johns is also is one of the few waterways in the world that flows north.

The boardwalk goes by a kayak landing and at about 3.1 miles arrives at a bad-weather shelter. This is the wilderness area's only primitive campsite. Past the campsite, the boardwalk continues to border the river until mile 4.0. There the trail turns left and leaves the St. Johns River behind. A levee now replaces the boardwalk.

For the next mile, the hike becomes rougher and tougher. The levee, while straight, is narrow and filled with tree roots. In places it's challenging to maintain your balance and not slither down the dirt mound—especially when the slope is almost a 45-degree angle.

Moving forward requires scrambling up and down the side of the big dirt mound, which is slick and slippery after a rain. This is why some locals consider the BBWA loop trail to be Central Florida's hardest hike.

The trail becomes boardwalk beside the St. Johns River.

Conditions ease up at about mile 5.15 when the trail goes left and descends onto a level forest road. A bench is available for taking a time-out. This forest road is a reliable place to spot Florida black bear, as the Black Bear Wilderness Area now borders other preserves. Deer and wild pigs are also often seen from the forest road.

The forest road passes some water-control equipment and crosses a few moving streams before the trail returns to the levee where the loop began. Turn right to retrace your steps to the trailhead parking lot.

Miles and Directions

0.0   Start at the Black Bear Wilderness trailhead.

0.15 The loop begins; go right.

0.9   The trail crosses a wide power line clearing.

1.0   First view of St. Johns River. (*Option:* Turn around here for an out-and-back hike of 2.0 miles.)

3.15 Arrive at primitive campsite and shelter.

4.0   The trail leaves the St. Johns River and goes left. From this point, the hike may be sloppy after rains.

7.05 Come to the end of the loop. Turn right.

7.1   Arrive back at the trailhead.

Little Big Econ State Forest

In Central Florida, river bluffs as high as these are unusual and may be the reason for the Econlockhatchee River's name, meaning "earth mound stream."

The Kolokee Trail is one of the region's best hikes for both waterway and wilderness scenery. While hiking here, it is possible to view bald eagles, ospreys, roseate spoonbills, and sandhill cranes. Deer and turkeys are also likely, and a Florida black bear is a real possibility if you hike early, just after sunrise.

The Econlockhatchee River, known simply as the "Econ," is a blackwater river (any slow-moving stream that flows through forested swamps or wetlands where the water is turned black by the tannic acid leached from fallen tree leaves) that meanders through some of the least-developed parts of Central Florida, a region where open spaces are scarce. The Econ is a designated Outstanding Florida Waterway, deemed worthy of special protection because of its natural attributes. It's called "Little" and "Big" Econ because the river's width dramatically varies in size. In some places the Econ is almost a narrow winding stream. In others it is broader and appears like a true, classic river.

Econ is a pronounceable abbreviation of the river's full name—Econlockhatchee—which is a mouthful. Pronounced "EE-con-lock-hatch-ee," it is a Muskogee word meaning "earth mound stream." That description is interpreted to mean that numerous man-made earthen mounds once existed along the river.

The Kolokee hike is named for the early 1900s railroad, turpentine, and sawmill town once located in this area. It became a ghost town when the Florida East Coast Railway ended service to it.

Although this hike is not listed under "Overnight Hikes," it should be considered a good candidate. There is a group camping area, as well as several smaller ones.

Start: Kiosk at the Barr Street parking lot

Distance: 5.3-mile loop

Difficulty: Easy to moderate, depending on whether the trail is muddy

Hiking time: 2–3 hours

Seasons: Nov through mid-May for the most comfortable and the driest months

Fees and permits: Day-use fee pass of $2. The pass must be purchased in advance. Call (877) 879-3859 or visit floridastateforests .reserveamerica.com. Primitive camping permit required.

Trail contact: Division of Forestry, Little Big Econ State Forest, 1350 Snow Hill Rd., Geneva 32732; (407) 971-3500; fdacs.gov/ Forest-Wildfire/Our-Forests/State-Forests/ Little-Big-Econ-State-Forest

Schedule: Day use from sunrise to sunset; visitor center hours: 8 a.m. to noon and 1 to 4 p.m., weekdays only

Dog-friendly: Leashed dogs permitted

Trail surface: Dirt path and footbridges

Land status: Florida state forest

Nearest town: Oviedo

Other trail users: Cyclists and equestrians have their own designated trails. The Kolokee Trail is limited to foot traffic, although it joins a multiuse trail.

Water availability: Bring your own; none available at the Barr Street trailhead

Maps: Available online; sometimes available at the parking lot information kiosk

Special considerations: If you get hurt or lost in the forest on the trail, call 911 and identify the white "Rescue Sign" number you are nearest. Hunting is permitted on a nearby tract but not in this section.

Camping: Camping is allowed by permit only. The West Camp along the Florida Trail loop has 5 primitive tent sites holding up to 6 people. A campsite for groups of up to 20 people is located about 0.3 mile from the trailhead; the farthest site is 0.78 mile from the trailhead. Campsites have no water, electricity, or restrooms. They do have a fire ring, picnic table, and lantern holder. The camping fee is $8.93 per person per night. Reserve and pay at floridastateforests.reserveamerica.com.

Amenities: Restroom in the visitor center located at 1350 Snow Hill Rd., Geneva

Cell service: Good

Trail conditions: Usually dry, this trail has some steep and rocky parts and areas of soft sand. This is not a wheelchair-accessible trail. The white-blazed return trail is shared with equestrians.

23 Kolokee Loop Trail

Distance: 5.3-mile lollipop loop

Finding the trailhead: The forest is located between the small towns of Chuluota and Geneva in eastern Seminole County. Coming from Geneva or Oviedo, take CR 426 (Oviedo Road) to Barr Street, 3.3 miles east of Oviedo. State forestry signs make the parking lot easily identifiable. There are no facilities at the Barr Street trailhead. Trailhead GPS: 28.687403 / -81.159278

Kolokee Loop Trail

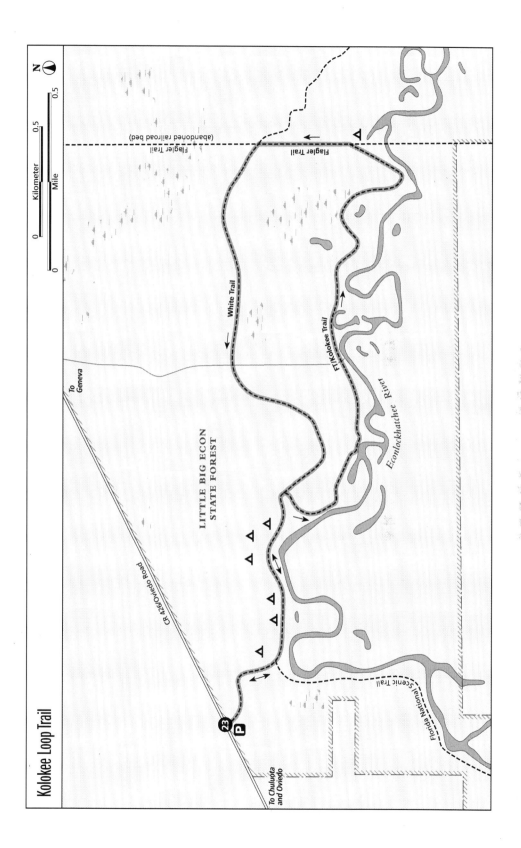

N

Kilometer · Mile
0   0.5
0   0.5

LITTLE BIG ECON STATE FOREST

White Trail

FT/Kolokee Trail

Flagler Trail

Flagler Trail (abandoned railroad bed)

Econlockhatchee River

Florida National Scenic Trail

CR 426/Oviedo Road

To Geneva

To Chuluota and Oviedo

23 P

The Hike

This hike goes through some of Central Florida's most remarkable, unspoiled scenery as the trail hugs the riverbank. With primitive campsites near the river, this is a good place for a weekend escape. Fishing from the riverbank is possible for anyone with a Florida freshwater fishing license.

The hike begins from the Barr Street parking lot. Hike the edge of an open field and follow the well-marked white-blazed access trail. In about 0.2 mile, intersect the orange-blazed Florida Trail. Take it and soon pass the group campground. You should be able to see the Econ on your right. It's possible to approach the river more closely than the trail, which keeps to high ground to avoid wet areas when the Econ is rain swollen.

The Kolokee Trail intersects the blue Flagler Trail. Follow this short connector to the white-blazed multiuse trail. Turn left on the white-blazed trail to return to the trailhead. You're now almost at the halfway point of the hike. To avoid cyclists and equestrians entirely, you must return the same way you came.

Another option is to go right, not left, on the white-blazed multiuse trail and hike 1.4-miles to the trailhead where the visitor center and the state forest office are also located. Some hikers prefer this route and arrange to be picked up or even start from there. *Note:* The forest office does not issue day-use passes; those need to be purchased online before arriving.

Miles and Directions

0.0 Start at the Barr Street parking lot and follow the white-blazed trail.

0.2 Junction with the orange-blazed Florida Trail; go straight on the FT.

0.3 Reach an open field and the West Camp designated camping area that parallels the Florida Trail.

1.1 Go right to start the Kolokee Loop on the Florida Trail.

2.4 The Kolokee Trail intersects the blue-blazed Flagler Trail; turn left.

2.8 The Flagler Trail intersects a white-blazed multiuse trail bicycle/equestrian trail. Turn left onto the white-blazed trail. (***Option:*** Going right will take you to the state forest main office on Snowhill Road. Some hikers like to add this section for a longer walk.)

4.1 Close the loop. Turn right to return to the orange-blazed Florida Trail and pass the open-field West Camp.

4.9 The Florida Trail intersects the white-blazed access trail to the Barr Street trailhead.

5.1 Arrive back at the Barr Street parking lot.

Split Oak Forest Wildlife and Environmental Area

The 1,700-acre Split Oak Forest Wildlife and Environmental Area (WEA) is named for a giant 200-year-old oak tree that split in the middle and, amazingly, continues to grow today. The forest borders two very picturesque lakes—Lakes Hart and Mary Jane.

Split Oak Forest is owned jointly by Orange and Osceola Counties. The Florida Fish and Wildlife Conservation Commission manages Split Oak Forest to protect the threatened upland species living here and to provide them with the best possible environment. Of particular concern is enhancing and preserving habitat for the gopher tortoise.

The property, however, is currently involved in a controversy surrounding Split Oak Forest's future. About 86 percent of Orange County residents voted to pass an amendment to their county's charter that would protect the popular forest from future development. Despite the land's supposed protected status, a state agency appeared to approve plans to chop down 160 acres of the forest so a new highway can be built through it. Regardless of how this is resolved, the hiking trails seem to be secure from development.

Split Oak Forest WEA features the 5.2-mile Split Oak Loop. On the North Loop, the Lake Loop spur offers a 0.9-mile hike bordering Lake Hart and Bonnett Pond. The 0.9-mile connector trail marking the dividing line for the North and South Loops accommodates those who would like to see the forest but not hike the entire trail.

The head of this stoic gopher tortoise is covered in mosquitoes, yet it doesn't seem bothered by them.

After leaving the Lake Loop, the North Loop intersects a connector trail leading to adjacent Moss Park. This Orange County park offers camping and usually hosts a large gathering of sandhill cranes in winter. The 0.8-mile connector path known as the Swamp Trail runs atop a berm and crosses a marsh. It provides quick and short access into Moss Park.

Although the South Loop doesn't offer as many options or lead to other places, it traditionally has more wildlife sightings and offers another chance to spot the wildlife found in Split Oak Forest, including coyotes (rare), alligators, wood storks, red-shouldered hawks, gray foxes, gopher tortoises, and box turtles. Sandhill cranes favor the prairie on the South Loop.

One of the management tools used to generate suitable wildlife habitat is controlled prescribed fire. Many wildlife species require their habitat to produce the kinds of foods they depend on. Instead of destruction, prescribed fires promote seed and fruit production as well as the new growth of flowering plants and shrubs. A burned forest may not look pretty to us, but to certain animals it's probably appetizing. Natural communities include scrub, hammocks, pine flatwoods, marshes, and swamps.

Start: Kiosk near the main parking area

Distance: Hiking the North, South, and Lake segments and using the 0.4-mile access trail twice makes for a hike of about 6.6 miles.

Difficulty: Easy to moderate. Areas of soft sand may require more effort. Depending on recent weather, parts of the trail could be muddy.

Hiking time: 1.5-2 hours for the featured hike

Seasons: Nov to May for the best weather

Fees and permits: No fees or permits required for day use; Florida license required for freshwater fishing

Trail contact: Moss Park (a nearby Orange County park), 12901 Moss Park Rd., Orlando 32832-6228; (352) 732-1225. Moss Park is located 4 miles southeast of CR 15 (Narcoossee Road) on Moss Park Road. The Split Oak Loop Trail is located on Clapp Simms Duda Road, Orlando. Parking and the hiking trail are the only facilities.

Schedule: Open 30 minutes before sunrise to 30 minutes after sunset year-round

Pet-friendly: Pets prohibited

Trail surface: Natural surface and boardwalk

Land status: Florida Wildlife and Environmental Area (WEA)

Nearest town: Narcoossee

Other trail users: Nature watchers

Water availability: No facilities; bring your own

Maps: Available at the trailhead and online at myfwc.com/media/29949/split-oak-trail-guide.pdf

Special considerations: Bicycles and firearms prohibited

Amenities: Restroom available at adjacent Moss Park

Cell service: Good

Trail conditions: Mostly sandy path, which may be soft in parts. This is usually an easy hike. The trail has a mix of sun and shade. Warm-weather hiking should be done early. Always have insect repellent.

24 Split Oak North and South Loops

Distance: 6.6-mile loop

Finding the trailhead: Split Oak Forest is located in Orange and Osceola Counties, approximately 16 miles south of Orlando. From Orlando International Airport, go east on SR 528 (Beeline Expressway) for 2.5 miles to exit 13. Go south on CR 15 (Narcoossee Road) for 7 miles. Turn east onto Clapp Simms Duda Road and follow signs to the entrance. Trailhead GPS: 28.353430 / -81.211078

The Hike

According to the Friends of Split Oak Forest, the former 7.7-mile Split Oak Loop has been reduced to 5.2 miles, with a notable loss of hiking trail on the South Loop. Both the North and South Loops are blazed in yellow. The western side of the North and South Loops is also marked with the orange blazes of the Florida Trail where it overlaps. Both blaze colors are visible when the two hikes share the trail.

The North Loop provides the only access to the 0.9-mile blue-blazed Lake Loop spur trail. Take the Lake Loop spur, which leads to Lake Hart; the trail borders it for a brief distance. The habitat in this section is classic to Central Florida, with cypress swamps, pine flatwoods, oak hammocks, and marshland. When the spur path turns to the right it parallels Bonnet Pond and its marked overlook. When the Lake Loop spur rejoins the North Loop, you are near the old split oak for which the park is named.

After the Florida Trail departs, the North Loop gradually curves south and intersects the South Loop at 3.3 miles. The South Loop typically is less used, but it has some of the best wildlife viewing, especially for sandhill cranes—the birds that make the rusty-hinge sound.

The South Loop has deep soft sand that slows down hiking. The trail goes south in an almost straight line until reaching the perimeter fence. There it turns right to follow the fence before heading south independently.

A spur trail from the right leads to a marshy area where you might spot wildlife. The South Loop next intersects the orange-blazed Florida Trail, coming from the south. The trail again has two different blazes. Keep an eye on those blazes, because in about 0.3 mile the trail makes an abrupt right. The trail then travels through a corridor of oaks before arriving at the access trail to the trailhead.

Miles and Directions

0.0 Start at the parking lot kiosk. Follow the 0.4-mile access trail, marked with both orange and yellow blazes.

0.4 The access trail intersects the North and South Loops. Go left to join the North Loop.

1.7 Turn left to join the 0.9-mile Lake Loop.

2.3 A side trail on the left leads to a platform overlooking Bonnett Pond.

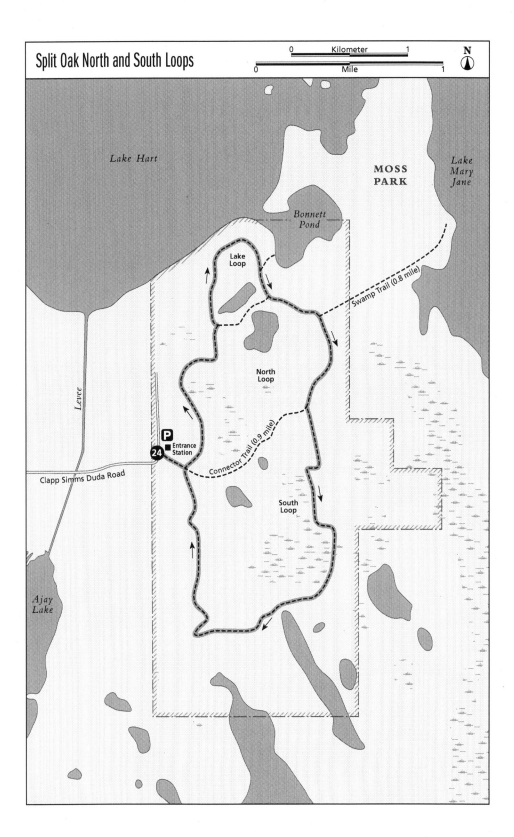

Split Oak North and South Loops

Lake Hart

MOSS PARK

Lake Mary Jane

Bonnett Pond

Lake Loop

Swamp Trail (0.8 mile)

North Loop

Connector Trail (0.9 mile)

Levee

Entrance Station

24

Clapp Simms Duda Road

South Loop

Ajay Lake

2.6 The Lake Loop ends as it rejoins the yellow and orange blazed North Loop. This junction marks the area of the great split oak for which the park is named. Go left onto the North Loop.

2.8 Coming in from the left, the 0.8-mile Swamp Trail leading to Moss Park intersects the North Loop. Stay on the North Loop, now with only yellow blazes. The Florida Trail is left behind as the trail now follows a berm leading into Moss Park.

3.3 The North Loop intersects the South Loop and the 0.9-mile center connector trail, which provides a shortcut back to the parking lot. From here, it is 1.3 miles back to the parking lot including the 0.4-mile connector trail.

4.0 The trail becomes deep sand, not the easiest hiking terrain.

4.3 The trail meets the perimeter fence; turn right to follow fence.

4.5 Check the view from a platform overlooking a marshy area.

5.2 The Florida Trail comes in from the south. The trail blazes are now both orange and yellow.

5.9 Walk through a corridor of impressive live oaks.

6.2 Reach junction with the access trail back to the trailhead; turn left.

6.6 Arrive back at the parking lot.

The Nature Conservancy's Disney Wilderness Preserve

Located only about 15 miles south of Walt Disney World, despite its name, the 11,500-acre Disney Wilderness Preserve is not part of the giant Disney complex. The property is owned and managed by The Nature Conservancy (TNC), which is in the process of returning the tract to its original wetlands condition. Disney's name is connected to the preserve only due to the Clean Water Act, which requires wetlands damaged by human activity to be mitigated (replaced) elsewhere.

The Disney Preserve is a mitigation project established in 1992 with an initial purchase of 8,500 acres. More acreage has since been added by other businesses needing to mitigate after disturbing a natural wetlands area. However, these companies haven't been added to the preserve's name, perhaps to their relief.

The Nature Conservancy believes the preserve is home to more than 1,000 species of plants and animals. These plants and animals could pop up anywhere along the hiking trails laid out on 700 acres near Lake Russell.

Unlike other Florida Disney-named lands, there are no drink stands, ice-cream vendors, or hot dog sellers anywhere about—and that's very, very nice. If you don't bring your own water, you will get thirsty on this sunny open trail. Because the trails have little shade from the intense sun, they are best hiked in the cooler months.

Start: The Nature Conservancy conservation learning center

Distance: Four loop trails with a perimeter of 5.3 miles; shorter hikes available

Difficulty: Because shade is sparse, hikes may be moderately difficult for young children and some adults. Everyone needs some kind of shade hat.

Hiking time: 2–3 hours

Seasons: Best in the dry, cooler months, generally Nov to May

Fees and permits: No admission fee; donations welcomed

Trail contact: The Disney Wilderness Preserve, 6075 Scrub Jay Trail, Kissimmee 34759; (407) 935-0002; nature.org/en-us/get-involved/how-to-help/places-we-protect/the-disney-wilderness-preserve/. Trails are sometimes closed due to flooding or restoration activities. Call ahead.

Schedule: TNC advises calling ahead to verify the schedule. Do not rely on Google's notation whether the preserve is open or closed; it is often incorrect. Normally the preserve is open 9 a.m. to 4:30 p.m., Mon to Fri, May through Oct; may also be open on Sat during this period. Also open weekends Nov to Apr; closed most major holidays.

Dog-friendly: Pets prohibited

Trail surface: Hard surface, dirt/sand paths, boardwalk

Land status: Privately owned by The Nature Conservancy

Nearest town: Poinciana

Other trail users: Hikers only; smoking prohibited on trails

Water availability: Limited to the visitor restrooms; best to bring your own

Maps: Available online and at the preserve

Amenities: Information center, restroom

Cell service: Good to fair

Trail conditions: Because this is a wetlands area, trails could be muddy during the rainy season. Many parts of the hike lack shade. Wear a hat, take water, and pack insect repellent.

Almost all the preserve's trails are in open sun and have little shade. Carrying a water bottle from home is essential.

25 Top of the Loop Trails

Distance: About 2.5-mile loop

Finding the trailhead: From I-4, take the SR 535 exit and go south to Poinciana Boulevard. Turn right (south) and go to the end of the road, about 15 miles, and turn right onto Pleasant Hill Road. Proceed approximately 0.25 mile, turn left onto Old Pleasant Hill Road, and go 0.5 mile to Scrub Jay Trail. Turn left and follow Scrub Jay Trail to The Nature Conservancy's Conservation Learning Center at Disney's Wilderness Preserve. Trailhead GPS: 28.129174 / -81.431239

The Hike

The preserve has four hiking trails, each blazed with a different color. The Harden Trail blazes are white, the Wilderness Trail is blazed in blue, the Red Trail has red blazes, and the Yellow Trail is blazed in yellow.

Three of the trails are grouped closely together at the top of the loop. For our purposes, those three trails have been combined to create the Top of the Loop hike, totaling about 2.5 miles. These are the most heavily used trails.

The first loop hike is the 0.5-mile Harden Loop, blazed in white. When you first arrive at the trailhead, you'll notice that the Harden Trail is on the right and the

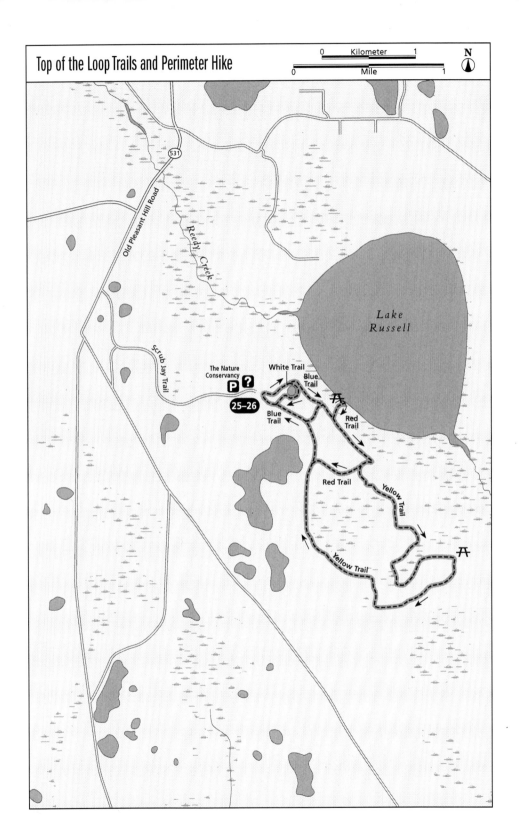

Kilometer

Mile

N

Old Pleasant Hill Road

531

Reedy Creek

Lake Russell

Scrub Jay Trail

The Nature Conservancy

P ?

25–26

White Trail

Blue Trail

Blue Trail

Red Trail

Red Trail

Yellow Trail

Yellow Trail

Wilderness Trail is straight ahead. You might think that you will return to this trail junction after completing the Harden Loop, but that is not the case.

The Harden Trail makes about a three-quarter loop around a cypress dome on a wide mowed path located a good distance from the trees. There is no opportunity to actually see inside the cypress dome from the trail. There should be considerable bird activity in the trees at the edge of the dome during certain times of year. Take binoculars to be able to see anything. Don't expect much activity on a hot day, when the birds enjoy the shade inside the dome.

A wet area prevents the Harden Trail hike from making a complete circuit of the cypress dome. As a result, the trail doesn't come out where you might expect—back at the joint trailhead for both the Harden and Wilderness Trails.

Instead, the Harden Trail emerges at T junction in a different location, where there are no obvious directions. The beautifully laid-out map in the preserve's brochure is of no help. Instead of signs, look for small posts with weathered metal discs containing colored arrows pointing in various directions.

Once you exit the cypress dome trail, going right takes you back to the access trail and the visitor center. Going left leads to the Wilderness, Red, and Yellow Trails. My suggestion: When the access trail from the visitor center brings you to the junction with both the Harden and Wilderness Trails, take the Wilderness Trail. It takes you places. The Harden Trail is a dead end; leave it until the end.

Begin the blue-blazed Wilderness Trail that parallels the shore of Lake Russell. After a junction with the Red Trail, prepare to go left onto the 0.1-mile spur trail leading to a picnic area on Lake Russell. Ringed with cypress trees, the 540-acre lake is one of the most northerly headwaters of the tropical Everglades, located hundreds of miles to the south.

When ready, return to the Red Trail and turn left. The forest around you is known as a longleaf pine savanna, found from Virginia to Texas. Today, more than 97 percent of all longleaf pines in the United States have been harvested.

The tall skinny trees, with needles up to 14 inches long, are adapted to fire and even rely on it to kill competing plants that overgrow longleaf seedlings. The longleaf pine forest here was revived with controlled prescribed fires that brought back the understory of saw palmetto and native grasses. Native Americans also burned forests to prepare them for farming, create animal habitat, and prevent large uncontrolled fires.

Longleaf pines are the only place where the rare and endangered red-cockaded woodpecker makes its home. A nesting pair of red-cockaded woodpeckers has been introduced into the preserve. You are more likely to hear than see them.

Just 0.7 mile after leaving Lake Russell, the Red Trail intersects the much longer Yellow Trail. You have the choice of remaining on the Red Trail or hiking the Yellow Trail for an additional 3.6 miles. If you remain on the Red Trail, once at the parking lot, you will have walked about 2.5 miles.

26 Perimeter Hike

Distance: 5.3-mile loop

Finding the trailhead: From I-4, take the SR 535 exit and go south to Poinciana Boulevard. Turn right (south) and go to the end of the road, about 15 miles, and turn right onto Pleasant Hill Road. Proceed approximately 0.25 mile, turn left onto Old Pleasant Hill Road, an go 0.5 mile to Scrub Jay Trail. Turn left and follow Scrub Jay Trail to The Nature Conservancy's Conservation Learning Center at Disney's Wilderness Preserve. Trailhead GPS: 28.129174 / -81.431239

The Hike

Adding the 3.6-mile Yellow Trail to the perimeter lengths of the Top of the Loop trails creates a hike of 5.3 miles. The Yellow Trail almost immediately passes a dome of cypress trees with clusters of white Spanish moss. This air plant is in the same family as the pineapple. Before synthetic cushioning was created, the moss was used to stuff automobile seats, couches, and mattresses and for home insulation. Today it's used mostly to decorate flowers and for mulch.

The trail passes several more seasonal lakes before entering a series of oak hammocks, eventually reaching a bench under one of the shade trees—a nice spot to relax and sip some water.

Going across the bottom of the loop, the trail veers sharply right to begin its return to the trailhead. A bayhead swamp remains off to the right but at a much greater distance. This huge marshland is part of the preserve's 3,500 acres of restored and protected wetlands. One reason these are so important is that they filter out nutrients and help replenish clean groundwater.

The trail passes between several deep depressions/seasonal lakes. Look for birds and deer here. Large white wood storks may visible be in the marshy wetlands. They also nest around Lake Russell.

Join a forest road and hike past a large swampy area on the right. Continue straight and arrive at a bench close to a junction with the Red Trail. Follow the Red Trail to return to the visitor center using the Wilderness and Harden Trails. If you don't spot deer from the hiking paths, don't give up hope. You're just as likely to see them bounding over the field as you drive to the entry gate. Bambi's children, your kids may claim. And why not?

Miles and Directions

0.0 Start from the trailhead at the visitor center.

0.2 At the joint trailhead for the Harden and Wilderness Trails, take the Wilderness Trail.

0.3 The trail splits. Go left on the Blue Trail and follow the "Lake Russell" sign.

0.4 Pass or take the 0.1-mile spur trail to Lake Russell. (**Note:** The lake is the place to be first thing in the morning for a chance to see otters and ospreys.)

1.7 About 0.7 mile after leaving the shore of Lake Russell, the Red Trail makes a sharp left just before it intersects the Yellow Trail. (***Option:*** Take the Red Trail to return to the parking lot for a loop walk of about 2.5 miles. The full hike is 3.1 miles longer.) Continue on the Yellow Trail.

2.0 On the Yellow Trail, pass a stand of oak trees and a shaded bench.

2.6 Make a sharp turn.

3.4 Come to a junction with a jeep trail and pass another bench.

4.0 Reach a junction with a spur trail to a picnic area.

4.2 The Red Trail ends at a junction with the blue-blazed Wilderness Trail. Continue straight to follow the Wilderness Trail back to the visitor center.

5.4 Arrive back at the visitor center.

Hillsborough River State Park

Although not very impressive, this is the largest set of rapids in Central Florida.

The 3,738-acre Hillsborough River State Park features several nature hikes and a scenic loop of just over 3 miles. The trails combine for a total of 7.3 miles through one of Florida's most scenic state parks. Shorter options, including our featured hike, are available.

The park is famous for its two small sets of rapids, created by outcrops of Suwannee Limestone. Although they are not a cause for excitement for most visitors, the chance to hear rapids while hiking is virtually unknown in Florida. These are ranked as Florida's only Class II rapids, but that rating seems generous. The river flows swiftly there, and swimming is not permitted.

About one-fourth of the park occupies lowland areas. During spring and summer rains, seasonal flooding may occur that impacts the hiking trails; plan accordingly. The featured 5.8-mile hike links the River Rapids, Baynard, and Seminole Trails.

The river plain and pine flatwoods near the Hillsborough River are home to deer, wild turkeys, pileated woodpeckers, red-shouldered hawks, and barred owls. A walk through the dense old-growth tree canopy beside the lively Hillsborough River is one of the most memorable jaunts in Florida. Although this hike is not listed with the "Overnight Hikes," the primitive campsite here is one to consider.

Start: Northeast corner of the parking lot

Distance: 5.8-mile lollipop, including a 3.2-mile loop

Difficulty: Mostly easy

Hiking time: About 3 hours

Seasons: Nov to mid-May for the best weather; often crowded in summer

Fees and permits: Park admission of $6 per vehicle

Trail contact: Hillsborough River State Park, 15402 US 301, Thonotosassa 33592; (813) 688-9500; floridastateparks.org/parks-and-trails/hillsborough-river-state-park

Schedule: Open daily, 8 a.m. until sunset

Dog-friendly: Leashed pets permitted

Trail surface: Natural surface, boardwalks

Land status: Florida state park

Nearest town: Thonotosassa

Other trail users: Nature lovers

Water availability: Available at restrooms and developed campsites

Maps: Available at the park entrance and online

Special considerations: Accessible facilities include picnic tables and grills, campsites with concrete pad, nearby restrooms, parking, and the interpretative center for Fort Foster Historic State Park.

Camping: RV and tent camping, with electricity available at most of the 112 campground sites. Fees are $24 per night plus tax, plus a nonrefundable $6.70 reservation fee and a $7 nightly utility fee, except for tent campers. Each site is equipped with water, a fire ring, and a picnic table. Restrooms have hot showers. Laundry facilities are available. The campground also has a dump station.

Glamping: Sleep in a tent with a bed and air-conditioning. The tent also has places to sit, eat, and charge your cell phone. Contact Timberline Glamping: (813) 586-3081; tampa.tlglamping.com.

Amenities: Picnic facilities with tables and grills, bicycle trails, kayaking, canoeing, fishing (Florida license required), and interpretative center for Fort Foster Historic State Park

Cell service: Good

Trail conditions: Many hikers are drawn to the short River Rapids Trail, which can be crowded on weekends. After rain, the Baynard Trail may have wet sections. The Seminole Trail is the best hike for seeing wildlife and getting away from the crowds. This trail has both dry sand and patches of mud.

27 River Rapids and Baynard Trails

Distance: About 1.5 miles

Finding the trailhead: Hillsborough River State Park is located 9 miles north of Tampa and 6 miles south of Zephyrhills on US 301. Park at the parking lot on the right, located several hundred yards after the turnoff to the Fort Foster Museum. Trailhead GPS: 28.140456 / -82.227282

Coming southbound from Ocala on I-75: Take exit 279 (SR 54) east to US 301. Travel south on US 301 for 6 miles; the park will be on your right.

Going north on I-75 from Tampa: Take exit 265 (Fowler Avenue) east to US 301. Travel north for 9 miles; the park will be on your left.

Traveling westbound on I-4: Take exit 10 to CR 579. Follow CR 579 north to US 301. Following the signs, go north 7 miles; the park will be on your left.

Traveling I-4 eastbound: Take exit 7 (be careful of the merges) and go north on US 301 for 14 miles; the park will be on your left.

River Rapids and Baynard Trails and Seminole Trail

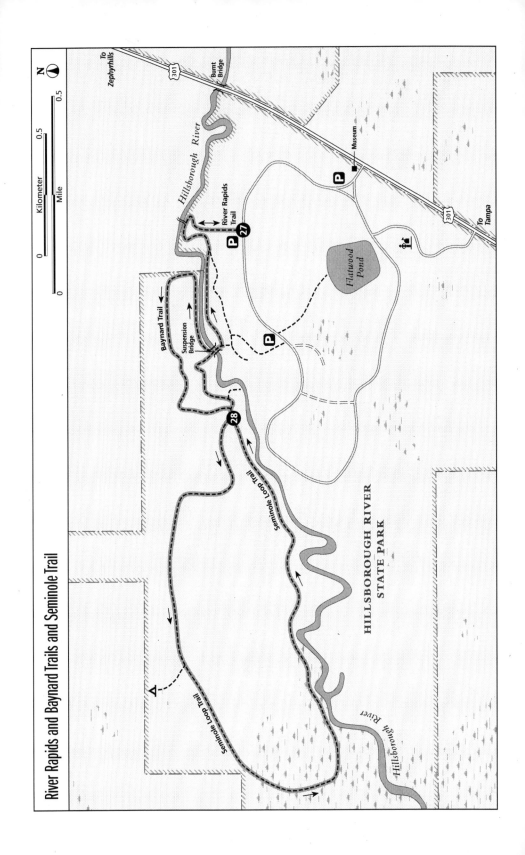

To Zephyrhills

301

Burnt Bridge

Hillsborough River

Museum

P

River Rapids Trail

P 27

Baynard Trail

Suspension Bridge

P

Flatwood Pond

28

Seminole Loop Trail

HILLSBOROUGH RIVER STATE PARK

Seminole Loop Trail

Hillsborough River

To Tampa

301

N

Kilometer
0   0.5

Mile
0   0.5

The Hike

From the trailhead, follow the River Rapids Trail's short 0.2-mile path that leads to the first set of rapids. This trail can be crowded with people clustering to see the rapids caused by a slight change in elevation.

With all the visitors, the path beside the river is well defined. It's impossible not to stop and take a photo in places. At about 0.3 mile, intersect a connector trail back to the trailhead from your left. Continue on a boardwalk going around a bend in the river. A short side path leads down to a huge cypress tree with many "knees."

Pass another River Rapids connector trail and at 0.6 mile arrive at the suspension bridge that will take you over the Hillsborough River. On the other side is the 1.1-mile Baynard Loop, named for the park's first superintendent.

After making the crossing, go right to enjoy a different perspective of the Hillsborough River from the opposite bank. In about 0.2 mile the trail turns left and goes inland to a section of forest that, depending on the season, alternates between wet and dry terrain. The Baynard Trail slowly curves back toward the river then intersects a 0.2-mile blue-blazed connector to the Seminole Trail, once part of the Florida Trail.

28 Seminole Trail

Distance: 3.2-mile loop

Finding the trailhead: Hike across the park suspension bridge accessing both the Baynard and Seminole Trails. Go left to join the Seminole Trail. Trailhead GPS: 28.140456 / -82.227282

The Hike

By hiking the River and Baynard Trails, you walked about 1.5 miles. Given the option, young hikers may prefer to spend more time along the river or visit the playground rather than hike the 3.2-mile Seminole Trail.

To return to the trailhead, take the Baynard Trail and return to the suspension bridge. Cross the river and either go to the playground or start retracing your steps to the trailhead on the River Rapids Trail.

To hike the Seminole Trail, follow the blue blazes for 0.2 mile and join the orange-blazed Seminole Trail for a 3.2-mile hike into the park's wilder areas. Animals you could find here are gopher tortoises, woodpeckers, owls, bobcats, and deer. After a mile, you'll reach a spur trail leading to a primitive campsite located on one of the trail's high and dryer spots.

Continuing, the trail yo-yos up and down, with stretches of both dry white sand and black mud. Footbridges cross areas that otherwise would be too messy to seriously contemplate. Eventually the trail starts back toward the Hillsborough River, reaching a small bluff above the waterway for a different river view.

From this point, the path follows the river for a short distance, passing over some feeder creeks. The trail turns away from the river and to a wet area with a series of footbridges that complete the trail. At the end of the Seminole Trail, the total hiking distance is about 5 miles.

Rejoin the blue-blazed access trail and turn right onto the Baynard Trail loop, which parallels the river before returning to the suspension bridge. From there you can take a shorter route back to the parking lot or retrace your initial River Rapids route.

Miles and Directions

0.0 Start at parking lot trailhead and follow the blue-blazed trail.

0.2 Reach a shelter and the first set of rapids; go left.

0.3 Cross a boardwalk over a cypress swamp.

0.6 Cross the river on a suspension bridge and turn right to start the Baynard Trail.

0.8 The trail turns inland.

1.5 Begin the Seminole Trail, going counterclockwise.

1.9 Reach a footbridge crossing a wet area.

2.5 Come to another footbridge and the junction with 0.1-mile blue-blazed trail to a primitive campsite. Stay on the orange-blazed trail.

3.0 Cross another wet area on a footbridge.

3.4 Emerge on a bluff overlooking the Hillsborough River.

4.0 Cross another footbridge.

4.8 End the Seminole Trail loop and join a new section of the Baynard Trail.

5.2 Return to the suspension bridge.

5.6 Return to the rapids.

5.8 Arrive back at the parking lot.

Tiger Creek Preserve

The Nature Conservancy (TNC) protects the 4,980-acre preserve bordering the edge of Florida's oldest and highest landmass, the venerable Lake Wales Ridge. Considered the most ancient part of Florida, the ridge is an enormous sand hill that runs north to south. This may have been the first place to emerge after the ocean covering the Florida peninsula receded. It is also possible that the narrow ridge was never covered by waves but stayed an isolated island where plants and animals evolved as the rest of the state was submerged.

Either scenario explains why the ridge contains one of the world's largest collections of rare plants and animals. According to the Conservancy, it has perhaps the highest concentration of rare and endangered plants in the continental United States. Animals residing here include sand skinks, gopher tortoises, the Florida mouse, indigo snakes, and gopher frogs. Rare plants include scrub plum, pygmy fringe tree, and Carter's mustard.

Established in 1971, the preserve is named for Tiger Creek, an unspoiled blackwater stream that cuts through the heart of the sanctuary. The land surrounding the waterway includes hardwood swamps, hammocks, oak scrub, pine flatwoods, sandhill, and longleaf pine–wiregrass habitat.

Tiger Creek has several hikes available. The Pfundstein Trail and Heron Pond Loop described here are among the most popular and easily accessed.

Start: Small parking area at the trailhead gate
Distance: 4.2 miles
Difficulty: Easy to moderate
Hiking time: 2–3 hours
Seasons: Dec to Apr for the best weather. This is a very dry and open area.
Fees and permits: None required
Trail contact: The Tiger Creek Center is open Mon through Fri, 9 a.m. to 5 p.m., except federal holidays. Call (863) 635-7506 for more information; nature.org/en-us/get-involved/how-to-help/places-we-protect/tiger-creek-preserve/
Schedule: Trail open daily during daylight hours
Pet-friendly: No pets permitted
Trail surface: Mostly natural, including sections of soft sand
Land status: Private preserve owned by The Nature Conservancy
Nearest town: Babson Park

Other trail users: Nature lovers
Water availability: None, bring your own
Maps: Available at the Pfundstein trailhead and online at the Tiger Creek website: nature.org/content/dam/tnc/nature/en/documents/tiger-creek-preserve-trail-map.pdf
Special considerations: Soft sand makes these trails inaccessible for those in wheelchairs.
Amenities: None
Cell service: Depends on how good your provider is in this remote area
Trail conditions: For the most part, the blazes are close together and in sight of one another, making this a very easy trail to follow. Trails consist of natural paths and forest roads. In a few places before Heron Pond, there are short sections with minor but noticeable elevation changes. In warm months the preserve's arid conditions can be similar to a desert. You need

The white-sand Pfundstein Trail leads into the heart of the preserve, where many rare animals and plants thrive.

to arrive with plenty of water and wear a wide-brimmed hat and sunglasses. The heat in this desert requires that you bring plenty of liquid for even the shortest hike. Without sunglasses, the glare off the bright white sand may give you a headache. Pack insect repellent, just in case.

29 Pfundstein Trail

Distance: 1.9 miles each way

Finding the trailhead: From the town of Babson Park, take SR 17 south for 2 miles. Turn left on North Lake Moody Road then left onto Murray Road. Go 2 miles and turn left onto Pfundstein Road. Go past a sign for the George Cooley Trail after you turn onto Pfundstein Road. The main parking area is several hundred yards ahead. Walk through the gate to access the trail. Trailhead GPS: 27.809087 / -81.484816

The Hike

The hike goes through a unique and irreplaceable habitat containing small remnants of ancient flora and fauna that used to be much more widespread. This property is considered the most famous and among the most important of Florida's ancient interior scrublands. An estimated forty plant and vertebrate species live here, including seventeen species listed for federal protection and over a dozen more proposed for federal listing as endangered or threatened.

Like the better-known Galapagos Islands, the ridge is composed of ancient beaches and sand dunes. Formed perhaps 1 to 3 million years ago, this region was sporadically isolated from North America by rising sea levels during ice ages. The plants and animals here were isolated for such long periods that some species developed differently than those on the mainland. The Nature Conservancy believes the preserve contains the highest concentrations of threatened and endangered plants and animals in the United States.

On this hike, it pays to be like Sherlock Holmes and pay attention to the tiniest details, such as the sand skink's winding tracks through the sand. This dry, open and sandy terrain is Florida's version of a desert. Ironically, this desert receives Florida's normal average 54 inches of rainfall, but the deep sand soaks up the water almost instantly.

Starting out, the white-blazed section of the Pfundstein Trail follows a bright white-sand trail through an area attempting to restore cutthroat grass, a species restricted to five Florida counties and found nowhere else in the world. The white sand gives way to deep sand in places, and oak hammocks characterize the next stretch of trail.

The white blazes are arranged so that they usually are in sight of one another. If at any point after making a turn to join another trail, the blazes seem to disappear, double-check which way the arrow points. If you are going in the proper direction, trust that a white blaze will appear shortly.

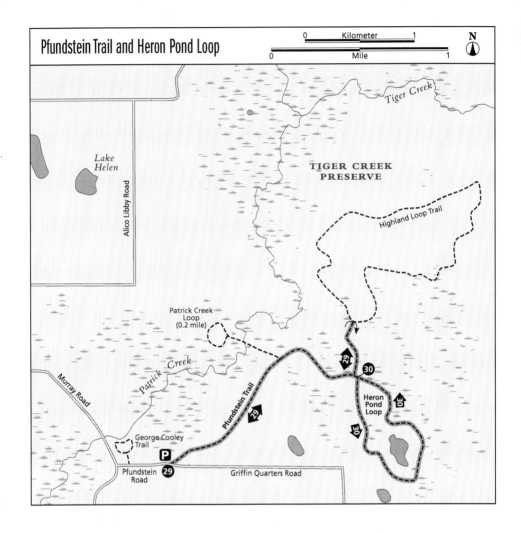

Kilometer

Mile

N

Tiger Creek

Lake Helen

Alico Libby Road

TIGER CREEK PRESERVE

Highland Loop Trail

Patrick Creek Loop (0.2 mile)

Murray Road

Patrick Creek

Pfundstein Trail

Heron Pond Loop

George Cooley Trail

Pfundstein Road

Griffin Quarters Road

At about 0.8 mile, a short side trail bears left to cross Patrick Creek, which has a tendency to flood. A short 0.2-mile side trail leads to a bridge over Patrick Creek. Assuming that the far bank hasn't been closed due to high water, the bridge leads to an often muddy 0.3-mile loop walk through marshland and dry hammock. After rejoining the Pfundstein Trail, turn left and in 0.7 mile reach the Heron Pond Loop.

30 Heron Pond Loop

Distance: 4.2 miles out and back

The red-blazed 1.2-mile Heron Pond Loop circles a pond that truly is an oasis for birdlife and other animals living in this parched desert.

Walking the trail counterclockwise, you'll encounter noticeable elevation changes. Ascend to the top of a small ridge where a bench overlooks Heron Pond. There is an even better pond view after you descend the hill, as the trail starts to circle Heron Pond.

Look for a side path on your left that leads to an observation platform with a good view of Heron Pond's open-water area. Continue on the loop trail as it curves around the pond. It climbs another ridge populated with scrubby flatwoods. More oaks and pines are located at the end of the Heron Pond Loop where it intersects the white-blazed Pfundstein Trail. Going left and returning to the trailhead is an out-and-back hike of 4.2 miles.

Miles and Directions

0.0   Start from the parking lot and follow the white blazes.

0.8   A blue-blazed 0.2-mile side trail to the left leads to a bridge crossing Patrick Creek and the 0.3-mile Great Sand Pine Loop. To continue to the Heron Loop, go straight.

1.5   Intersect the red-blazed Heron Pond Trail; go right.

1.9   The trail starts to loop around Heron Pond.

2.7   Reach a junction with the Pfundstein Trail; turn left to return to the trailhead.

4.2   Arrive back at the trailhead.

Prairie Lakes Unit–Three Lakes Wildlife Management Area

The 8,000-acre Prairie Lakes Unit is the midsection of the 63,500-acre Three Lakes Wildlife Management Area. Squeezed in between Three Lakes North and Three Lakes South, it includes a significant portion of the Kissimmee Prairie, one of the largest remaining dry prairies in Florida.

But this so-called "dry" prairie landscape, unique to southcentral Florida, doesn't stay permanently dry. Parts of dry prairies are often wet, and during the summer rainy season, shallow water may actually flow across the land like an incoming tide. The Prairie Lakes Unit was established to protect and manage wet prairies and marshes and to minimize their flooding damage. The best time to hike here is during drier and cooler periods.

Despite its remoteness, the Prairie Lakes Unit has two popular stacked loop trails offering different experiences. These trails are sometimes called the Lake Jackson and Lake Marian Double Loop. Each is about 5.5 miles. They are the perfect length for day hikes and also offer a good excuse to stay overnight.

If you have time for only one loop, make it the South Loop. The trail completely encircles a large area of dry prairie and borders several cypress swamps. It also has a 0.4-mile spur leading to a three-story tower overlooking Lake Jackson. The South Loop also offers several primitive campsites requiring advance reservations. Although Prairie Lakes is not listed with "Overnight Hikes," this location definitely is worth considering.

Prairie Lakes affords excellent bird-watching. It has at least seventy-five bald eagle nests, considered one of the largest nest concentrations anywhere in the Southeast. Look for nests in areas between Lake Jackson and Lake Marian, especially around Lake Marian. The adjoining section of Three Lakes WMA also contains numerous nests. See eagle nest locations here: cbop.audubon.org/conservation/about-eaglewatch-program.

Plants and animals living in the dry prairies are dependent on fire. Prescribed burns usually are done here between January and August.

Start: Parking lot at the trailhead of the North Loop, at the North Canal, or at the Lake Jackson parking area

Distance: North Loop, 5.5-mile loop; South Loop, 5.6-mile loop

Difficulty: Easy to moderate, depending on wetness

Hiking time: North Loop, 2-3 hours; South Loop, 2-3 hours

Seasons: Nov to mid-April for the coolest and driest weather

Fees and permits: No fees or permits required for thru-hikers; day-use permit of $3 or wildlife management area permit required

Trail contact: Florida Fish and Wildlife Conservation Commission, Northeast Region, 1239 Southwest Tenth St., Ocala 32674; (352) 732-1225; myfwc.com/about/

Schedule: Open daily, dawn until sunset

Dog-friendly: Pets prohibited

Trail surface: Primarily natural surface

Land status: Florida wildlife management area

Nearest town: Kenansville

Other trail users: Hunters in season

Water availability: There is no potable water; bring your own. If you're camping, have a water filter to tap Lake Jackson.

Maps: Available online from the Florida Fish and Wildlife Conservation Commission at store .avenza.com/products/three-lakes-wma -prairie-lakes-unit-brochure-map-florida-fish-an d-wildlife-conservation-commission-map; also the FWC's Three Lakes recreation guide: myfwc .com/media/26819/threelakes_recguide.pdf

Special considerations: During hunting season, hikers should wear 500 square inches of blaze-orange clothing above the waist; it must be visible in both front and back. The Florida hunting schedule is available at myfwc.com/ hunting/season-dates/. The hiking trails are not considered wheelchair accessible.

Camping: Except for during quota hunting season, camping is allowed by permit at designated primitive campsites on a first-come,

first-served basis. Camping is allowed during small game hunting season. Obtain a free camping permit from the FWC at (352) 732-1225. The camping locations are marked "B"- "E" on the Prairie Lakes brochure. They include campsites at Parker Hammock, Lake Jackson, and Dry Pond, all located on the South Loop. Parking is available at Lake Jackson at the end of Boat Ramp Road, the spur trail to Lake Jackson, and the designated area at the North Canal.

Amenities: Primitive campsites, vault toilets; no potable water available

Cell service: May be spotty

Trail conditions: Outside the rainy season, the well-marked trails are mostly dry and interspersed with areas of moist ground often covered by boardwalk. Hiking in the rainy season is a different situation when the dry prairies become wet. Wear appropriate footwear then, and be prepared to do some wading. Don't forget the insect repellent.

31 North Loop Trail

Distance: 5.5-mile loop

Finding the trailhead: From Kenansville, take SR 523 (Canoe Creek Road) for 9.5 miles to the Prairie Lakes Unit. Turn south onto Prairie Lakes Road. The parking area for the North Loop is located on the right, just off Prairie Lakes Road. Parking for the South Loop is available at the designated area at the North Canal. Trailhead GPS: 27.927654 / -81.124912

Hiking clockwise on the North Loop, the trail skirts cypress ponds where bald eagles frequently nest. Florida's bald eagles nest at a time contrary to that in other parts of the country. Elsewhere, bald eagles nest in spring and summer because food is at its most abundant during that time. Florida eagles, on the other hand, nest during Florida's dry winter, when prey is the most accessible. The dry cooler months are also best for hiking.

The North Loop has a slightly more diverse landscape. It features not only dry prairie but also cypress swamps with their famous domes and pine flatwoods where tall trees stand above wire grass, wildflowers, and saw palmettos.

Starting out, the North Loop borders an area with widely spaced pine trees. It then approaches a forest of cypress and uses a boardwalk to enter the Pole Cypress

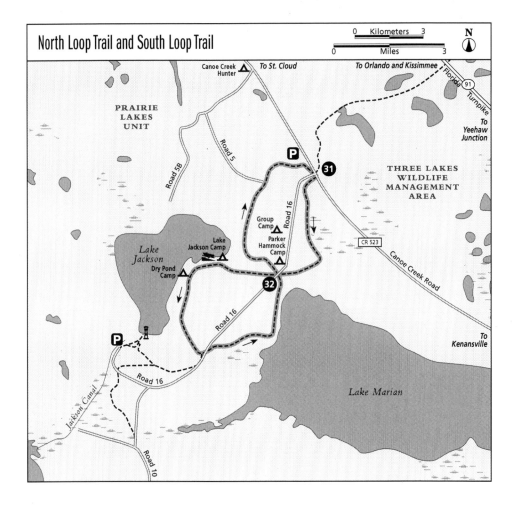

North Loop Trail and South Loop Trail

Kilometers 3

Miles 3

N

PRAIRIE LAKES UNIT

Canoe Creek Hunter

To St. Cloud

To Orlando and Kissimmee

Florida Turnpike 91

To Yeehaw Junction

Road 5B

Road 5

P

31

THREE LAKES WILDLIFE MANAGEMENT AREA

Road 16

Group Camp

Lake Jackson Camp

Parker Hammock Camp

CR 523

Lake Jackson

Dry Pond Camp

Canoe Creek Road

32

To Kenansville

P

Road 16

Road 16

Jackson Canal

Lake Marian

Road 10

Ponds swamp. From there the hike penetrates a mature pine flatwood, passes a fire tower, and goes under a power line. At about 1.5 miles it enters a hammock of large old oaks then crosses a sand road. The trail enters another oak hammock before arriving at the North Canal, using a connector between Lake Jackson and Lake Marian. At about 2.2 miles the trail crosses the entrance road, known as both the Prairie Lake Road and Road 16.

The trail also intersects here with a section of the South Loop that also has orange FT blazes. Although it is possible at this point to join the South Loop, this description is for the remainder of the North Loop. Going north, a short spur leads to the shaded Parker Hammock campsite, which has a bench and an old-fashioned pitcher pump. The trail borders Parker Hammock then enters scrubby flatwoods. At about 2.9 miles a sign points right, to the group camp with a vault toilet.

The trail stays in the shade as it passes dry prairie. At about 3.6 miles the trail follows a fence for a short distance; it then takes to the high ground above Parker

Slough. After crossing a bridge, the trail descends to the floodplain and, at 4.4 miles, reaches a picnic table.

The trail gradually turns right as it skirts the border of a pine savanna. On the right is a depression, which is a seasonal lake. The dry depression usually stays that way outside of the rainy season. Now it's time to circle the top of the North Loop Trail and arrive back at the parking lot at 5.5 miles.

Miles and Directions

0.0   Start from the North Loop parking lot. This section is part of the Florida Trail thru-hike.

0.4   Pass a high-water area.

1.5   Pass the road to a fire tower.

2.2   The North Loop intersects the South Loop; go right to continue on the North Loop.

2.9   A sign points right to the group camp with a vault toilet.

3.6   The trail follows a fence for a short distance.

4.4   The trail passes a picnic table.

5.5   Arrive back at the North Loop parking lot.

32 South Loop Trail

Distance: 5.6-mile loop

Finding the trailhead: Take SR 523 (Canoe Creek Road) to the Prairie Lakes Unit. Turn south onto Prairie Lakes Road. Parking for the South Loop is at the designated area at the North Canal. Trailhead GPS: 27.927654 / -81.124912

To begin the South Loop, cross the bridge at the North Canal and follow the orange FT blazes. The trail crosses a culvert and enters a hammock of oaks and palms then bypasses an area of wetlands. At 1.1 miles it crosses Boat Ramp Road, which goes to Lake Jackson. The trail parallels the road until entering a hammock. At 1.7 miles a sign points to the Dry Pond campsite.

The hike continues into a section of grassy dry prairie then enters a dense palm hammock before crossing a wooden bridge and following a berm. A bench at 2.4 miles is close to the midpoint of the South Loop. At this point, the Florida Trail exits the South Loop Trail. The South Loop is now blazed in white as it gradually turns north.

The short Lake Marian spur leads to an observation platform. I recommend taking it. The platform is not a high tower, but it gives you another opportunity to spot a bald eagle nest. Then continue north and cross Prairie Lakes Road/Road 16 a final time. The South Loop ends at 5.3 miles in front of the bridge and close to the North Canal parking area.

Miles and Directions

0.0 Start on the South Loop Trail.

1.1 Cross Boat Ramp Road.

1.7 Pass the Dry Pond campsite.

3.2 Blazes turn white when the Florida Trail turns south.

3.8 A footbridge crosses the South Canal; the trail turns north.

4.5 A sign points to the Lake Marian observation platform.

5.3 The South Loop ends in front of the canal bridge.

5.6 Arrive back at the North Canal parking area.

More Information

Access the three-story **Lake Jackson observation tower** by driving to the parking area at the end of Road 16. The 0.5-mile Lake Jackson Spur intersects the 0.3-mile Lake Jackson Tower Trail. The three-story tower provides a nice panoramic view of the lake. Buzzards also like to hang out there, and it's possible you will discover poopy signs of their presence.

The **Sunset Ranch**, another part of the Three Lakes WMA, is located just east of the Prairie Lakes Unit entrance. It features a 1.5-mile hike to Lake Marian, which has one of the largest concentrations of nesting bald eagles in the country. The lake edge is a good place to look for the nesting birds from January to May. Open daily sunrise to sunset. For more information check out myfwc.com/media/26797/sunset-ranch -trail-guide.pdf.

Little Manatee River State Park

The Little Manatee River Loop is an easy 6.5-mile walk that makes a nice, short stop on Florida's west coast. The Little Manatee River is a designated Florida Outstanding Water and part of the Cockroach Bay Aquatic Preserve. Yes, Florida names places for cockroaches—and pretty much anything else.

The Little Manatee River divides the 2,400-acre park into two sections. The southern section has a developed campground, horse trails, and a canoe launch. This is the section most people visit.

The northern section is open only to controlled foot traffic. Hikers must stop at the ranger station (open at 8 a.m.) to get the lock combination to enter the parking area at the hike's trailhead.

The Little Manatee is notable as one of southwest Florida's most pristine blackwater rivers. "Blackwater" is not a negative term but refers to any slow-moving stream that flows through forested swamps or wetlands where the water is turned black by the tannic acid leached from fallen tree leaves. The water quality of the Little Manatee is not impacted by the tannins.

Start: North Trail parking lot, located 3 miles north of the park's main facilities on US 301

Distance: 6.5 miles

Difficulty: Easy

Hiking time: 2-3 hours

Seasons: Dec to the end of Apr for the best weather

Fees and permits: Admission fee of $5 per vehicle; primitive camping, $5 per person plus tax

Trail contact: Little Manatee River State Park, 215 Lightfoot Rd., Wimauma 33598; (813) 671-5005; floridastateparks.org/parks-and-trails/little-manatee-river-state-park

Schedule: Open daily, 8 a.m. until sunset

Dog-friendly: Leashed pets allowed most places but not at the primitive campsites

Trail surface: Dirt, sand, and boardwalks

Land status: Florida state park

Nearest town: Wimauma

Other trail users: Nature watchers

Water availability: Bring your own for a hike. Filter river water if you plan to camp here.

Maps: Available at the entrance station

Special considerations: The park's southern section offers accessible parking and accessible campsites with a picnic table, ground grill, and nearby restroom.

Camping: Primitive backpacking on the Little Manatee River Loop trail is $5 per adult plus tax, $1 plus tax for those under 18. Backpackers must reserve their site in advance, check in at the main park, and arrive at least 2 hours before sunset to make sure they have time to reach their site and set up before dark. The park's campground loop has 30 sites for tents and RVs. Reserve up to 11 months in advance at reserve.floridastateparks.org/web/.

Amenities: Restrooms, campground, picnic facilities with tables and grills, hiking and equestrian trails

Cell service: Good

Trail conditions: This should be an easy hike unless you encounter slick boardwalk. Bring insect repellent.

A red-tailed hawk looks for its next meal.

33 Little Manatee River Loop

Distance: 6.5-mile loop

Finding the trailhead: Take the Sun City Center exit from I-75; go east on SR 674 to US Highway 301 and head south. Look for the park signs. The trailhead is on US 301, 3 miles north of the park main entrance. Trailhead GPS: 27.675498 / -82.348897

The Hike

About one-third of the walk borders the Little Manatee River. The rest meanders through sand pine, palmetto, oak hammocks, and oxbow wetlands, which store water that might otherwise lead to flooding. Wild azaleas along the trail make this a colorful route in February and March. Human intrusion here is limited, so you may see white-tailed deer, turkeys, foxes, bobcats, or scrub jays—possibly an alligator sunning itself.

Entrance to the parking lot for the hiking trail is across from Saffold Road, 3 miles north of the park's main entrance. Display proof of day-use payment on your dashboard. A short 0.25-mile access trail leads to the 6.5-mile loop blazed in white. FTA volunteers put a lot of effort into building the trail, which has more than twenty boardwalks and bridges.

The path from the parking lot parallels a fence before reaching an information kiosk explaining that although the hike is not part of the official Florida Trail, volunteers from the FTA's Suncoast chapter maintain it.

Take the boardwalk into a swampy section. At about 0.25 mile the boardwalk T's and the loop trail begins. Do the loop counterclockwise so you can hike beside the Little Manatee River on your return leg. Go straight into an upland forest, crossing a forest road at almost 0.5 mile. Then take a bridge across a creek. After a series of boardwalks and marshy conditions, the trail enters pine flatwoods and then scrubby oaks, where the trail turns to sand.

At 1.1 miles you have the opportunity to cut the hike from 6.5 miles to only 3 miles by taking a blue-blazed cross trail back to the trailhead. Continuing on the full loop, the trail descends to cross Cypress Creek at 1.5 miles. Cypress Creek is clear enough to see its sandy bed.

At 2.4 miles, pass a 0.2-mile blue-blazed access trail leading to a wooded area with a primitive campsite outfitted with a picnic table and fire ring. Continuing past the camp, the trail stays in the forest, but sounds of distant traffic on I-75 remind you that the trail isn't as remote as it might seem.

The trail turns left and descends toward the Little Manatee River. At 3.7 miles you finally arrive at the waterway. Enjoy a good view of the river from a sand bluff overlook.

From this point, the trail parallels the river's path much of the time. In spring and summer, manatees sometimes visit the area, but you'd be very lucky to see one. However, you might see a few kayakers, even an alligator.

Walking the next section, look up in the trees for air plants (bromeliads). Also look down to find seven sisters, swamp lilies with large white flowers.

After crossing a bridge and climbing a steep hill, the trail starts shadowing Cypress Creek, a Little Manatee tributary. At 4.6 miles the trail again intersects the blue-blazed cross trail. At 6.0 miles the trail leaves the Little Manatee River behind. From there, it's a short walk of 0.5 mile to the access path and the parking lot.

Miles and Directions

0.0 Start from the North Trail trailhead, across from Saffold Road.

0.25 The loop trail begins; go counterclockwise.

1.1 Intersect a blue-blazed cross trail. (*Option:* Take this trail back to the trailhead to shorten the hike to 3.0 miles.)

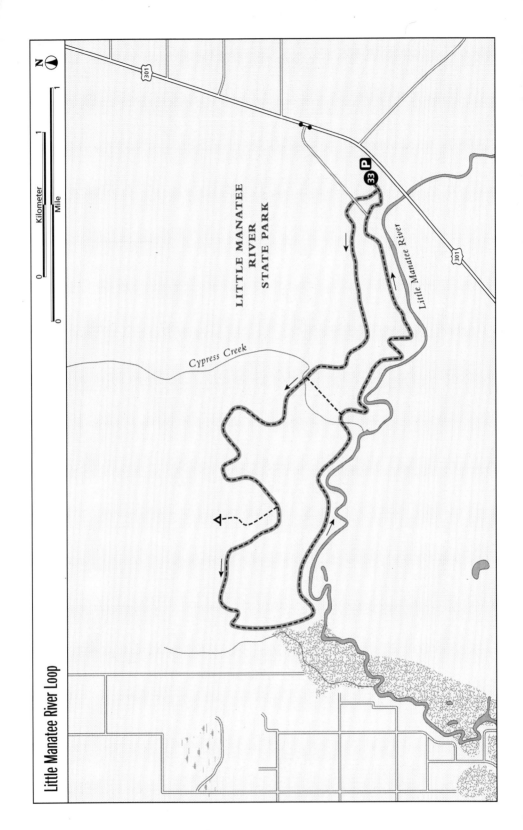

Little Manatee River Loop

1.15 Cross Cypress Creek.

2.4 Pass a spur trail to a primitive campsite.

3.7 Arrive at the Little Manatee River.

4.6 The trail again intersects the blue-blazed cross trail.

6.0 Leave the Little Manatee River behind.

6.5 Arrive back at the trailhead.

Overnight Hikes

Seminole State Forest

Seminole State Forest is located only 5 miles from I-4, Florida's most congested highway and the third most congested in the country. Even locals are surprised to learn there is a forest so close to the highway, with turkeys, white-tailed deer, sandhill cranes, alligators, turtles, eastern indigo snakes, otters, scrub jays, and quite a few Florida black bears.

Seminole State Forest is a slice of the authentic Florida many people know little about, and many believe no longer exists here since Central Florida is among the world's top travel destinations.

The 28,629-acre Seminole State Forest has more than 30 miles of hiking trails. They explore the Wekiva River Basin's uplands, wetlands, and riverine habitats inside a vital wildlife corridor connecting thousands of acres of publicly owned conservation lands leading to Ocala National Forest. Wildlife viewing here can be exceptional, including Florida black bears, which use this corridor regularly to move in and out of the region.

The first featured hike is a 7.5-mile section of the Florida Trail running north–south through the length of Seminole State Forest. The Lower Wekiva Loop Trail hike visits an area of the Wekiva Basin bordering the Wekiva River and Blackwater Creek.

Start: For both the Florida Trail and the Lower Wekiva Loop Trail, the hike begins from the parking lot at the southern end of the forest at the Bear Pond trailhead.

Distance: 7.5 miles one-way for the Florida Trail segment; 10.7 miles for the Lower Wekiva Loop Trail

Difficulty: Easy to moderate, depending on rainfall

Hiking time: 3–4 hours for the Florida Trail segment; 3–4 hours for the Lower Wekiva Loop Trail

Seasons: Nov to mid-May for the most pleasant hiking and camping

Fees and permits: The $2 day-use pass must be purchased online before visiting at florida stateforests.reserveamerica.com.

Trail contact: Lake Forestry Station, 9610 CR 44, Leesburg 34788; (352) 360-6675; fdacs.gov/Forest-Wildfire/Our-Forests/State-Forests/Seminole-State-Forest

Schedule: State forest open 24/7; day use from sunrise to sunset

Dog-friendly: Leashed dogs permitted

Trail surface: Mostly dirt or sand path, some boardwalk

Land status: Florida state forest

Nearest town: Sanford

Other trail users: Hunters on some forest trails in season

Water availability: Bring your own unless you plan to filter water from Bear Pond.

Maps: Available on-site and online

Special considerations: No swimming is permitted in the state forest. Portions of Seminole State Forest are managed as a wildlife management area (WMA) by the Florida Fish and Wildlife Conservation Commission (FWC). This means that when annual quota hunts take place, trails are closed to hikers for several days at a time.

Bear aware: Because of the sizable bear population, you should strongly consider using a bear canister or bear bag to store your food when camping.

Bear Pond is the common trailhead for both Seminole State Forest hikes.

Camping: There are 4 primitive campsites along the main Florida Trail hike. A permit is needed for overnight parking at the Bear Pond or Cassia trailhead; call (352) 584-1762. Make reservations online at floridastateforests .reserveamerica.com or call (877) 879-3859. **Amenities:** Vault toilets at the trailheads. The visitor center is located at 28500 SR 44, Eustis; (352) 589-1762.

Cell service: Good in parking lots but may be spotty in areas of thick forest
Trail conditions: The Florida Trail segment normally is easy when dry. The rainy season changes trail conditions into soggy walking. Dress appropriately. Mosquitoes and ticks can be unpleasant in warmer weather. Consider applying insect repellent before the hike as well as during it.

34 Florida Linear Out and Back Trail

Distance: 7.5 miles one way

Finding the trailhead: Access to the north–south running Florida Trail is available at two points. The southern trailhead is off SR 46, about 14 miles west of Sanford. From I-4, take the 101C exit and go west on SR 46. Access to the forest is on the right after crossing the Wekiva River. Arrive at the Bear Pond trailhead, the starting point for both hikes.

To reach the north trailhead, continue on SR 46 past the southern trailhead, then turn right onto SR 46A, which ends at CR 44. Go right onto CR 44 through the town of Cassia. The northern parking area will be on the right. Trailhead GPS: 28.8191923 / -81.428079

The Hike

The point-to-point hike starts from the Bear Pond trailhead and ends at the forest's north entrance in Cassia. The 7.5-mile hike goes through sand pine scrub, which provides ideal habitat for many threatened species, including the scrub jay, eastern indigo snake, hooded pitcher plant, and scrub holly.

From the Bear Pond trailhead off SR 46, follow the orange blazes. At 0.5 mile the trail crosses a footbridge. At 0.7 mile it passes Shelter Camp, which has not only a shelter but also space for camping. In a few more steps the trail reaches a Y junction with the white-blazed Lower Wekiva Loop Trail. Go left and follow the orange blazes to continue on the FT.

At 2.2 miles, the trail crosses East Spur Road and enters a large prairie. At 3.6 miles it intersects the Lower Wekiva Loop Trail, which uses the Florida Trail for its return to the Bear Pond trailhead.

After crossing Black Water Creek at 3.9 miles, the trail joins Pine Road and passes Sulphur Camp at 5.2 miles. The trail now turns right, going downhill to follow Palatka Road.

The white-blazed Cassia Spur trail intersects the Florida Trail as it makes a sharp right turn. Go left to finish the hike on the white-blazed trail. Due to rerouting, the Florida Trail now bypasses the Cassia trailhead.

The Cassia Spur enters thick palmetto before reaching a more open area near Boggy Creek Lake. To this point, you've hiked about 6.5 miles. On the final mile, skirt a large prairie before meeting more saw palmetto.

The trail curves around a depression known as Dead Cow Sink and Dead Horse Sink and then moves uphill to complete the 7.5-mile hike. If you didn't arrange for a shuttle or pickup, you'll need to retrace your steps to the Bear Pond trailhead for a 15-mile out-and-back hike. Reserving one of the primitive campsites in advance will make for a more relaxing return hike. Sulphur Camp is the first on the way back; its location also provides the opportunity to hike the Sulphur Loop trail.

Miles and Directions

The following directions are south to north.

0.0 Start at the marked fence near the trailhead kiosk.

0.5 Cross a footbridge.

0.7 Pass the Shelter Camp and a large tent camping area.

0.8 Intersect the white-blazed Lower Wekiva Loop Trail. Go left to stay on the orange-blazed FT.

2.2 Cross East Spur Road.

3.0 Cross the graded Sand Road.

3.6 Intersect the white-blazed Lower Wekiva Loop Trail, which joins the FT from the right to complete its loop by going south. Stay north on the orange-blazed trail.

3.7 Reach the blue-blazed side trail to the Blackwater Creek campsite (500 feet).

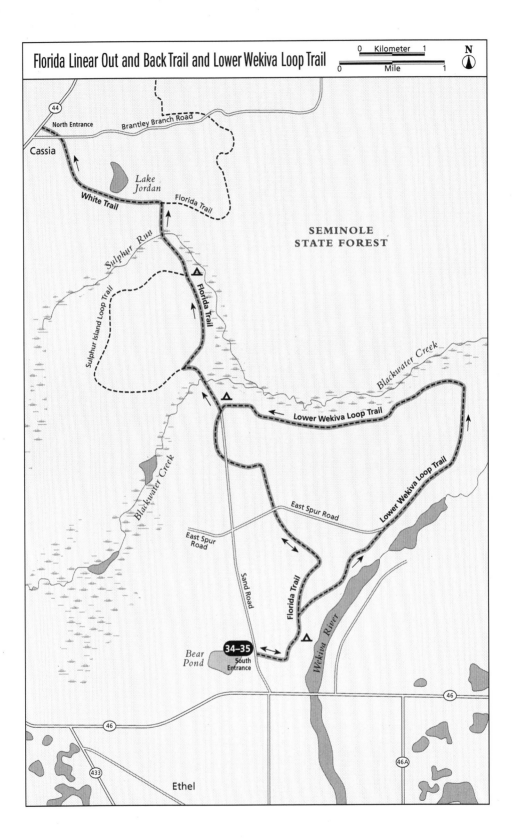

Florida Linear Out and Back Trail and Lower Wekiva Loop Trail

0 Kilometer 1
0 Mile 1

N

44
North Entrance
Brantley Branch Road

Cassia

Lake
Jordan

White Trail

Florida Trail

SEMINOLE
STATE FOREST

Sulphur Run

Sulphur Island Loop Trail

Florida Trail

Blackwater Creek

Lower Wekiva Loop Trail

Lower Wekiva Loop Trail

Blackwater Creek

East Spur Road

East Spur
Road

Sand Road

Florida Trail

Wekiva River

34–35
South
Entrance

Bear
Pond

46

46

433

Ethel

46A

3.9 Cross Blackwater Creek on a bridge.

4.1 Reach the junction of Sand and Grade Roads. Turn right onto Grade Road.

4.8 Cross Pine Road.

5.8 Intersect Palatka Road. Go right to follow Sand Road.

5.9 Join the white-blazed Cassia Spur trail.

7.3 Pass through a fence.

7.4 Pass Dead Cow/Horse Sink.

7.5 Arrive at the Cassia trailhead, the hike's northern parking lot.

35   Lower Wekiva Loop Trail

Distance: 10.7-mile loop

Finding the trailhead: From I-4, take the 101C exit and go west on SR 46. Access to the forest is on the right after crossing the Wekiva River. Arrive at the Bear Pond trailhead, the starting point for both Seminole State Forest hikes. Trailhead GPS: 28.8191923 / -81.428079

The Hike

This 10.7-mile loop includes the bonus of almost 4 miles on the Florida Trail. This scenic hike is highly recommended. From the Bear Pond trailhead, pass through the gate fence and use the orange blazes of the FT as an access trail. Cross a footbridge at 0.5 mile. At 0.7 mile pass the Shelter Camp, which provides a shelter and tent camping space.

The Florida Trail arrives at a Y junction with the white-blazed Lower Wekiva Loop Trail. Go right to join the white-blazed Lower Wekiva Loop Trail.

The forest now becomes denser, and the pines and cypress grow taller. In the distance, trees defining the border of the Wekiva River obscure the waterway. Pass a fork in the trail, and at 2.0 miles pass an intersection with a trail coming in from the left. After a bit of up-and-down walking, the trail ascends an old tramway, where you'll be looking down on the tops of smaller trees.

After climbing down the tramway, the trail passes giant mossy roots of old cabbage palms. Take the footbridge over a stream flowing into the Wekiva River. At 3.0 miles, pass through pine scrub. The trail then starts descending onto the Black Water Creek floodplain.

A blue-blazed side trail leads to Pine Lily Camp at 3.7 miles. Beyond this junction, the trail is a boardwalk set beside a forest road. At 4.4 miles the trail makes a sharp left into a hammock near Blackwater Creek. This is a more humid environment; look for bromeliads (air plants) in the trees.

After crossing a bridge, the trail enters a hammock where the path becomes increasingly wide as it moves from oak into pine flatwoods. At 5.1 miles it intersects a yellow-blazed equestrian trail leading to East Spur Road. (*Option:* Follow the equestrian trail to trim the hike from 10.7 miles to 8.8 miles.)

For the complete loop, stay with the white blazes. After following the border of a flatwoods forest, the path reaches a T junction at 6.9 miles with the Florida Trail on Sand Road, sometimes referred to as Main Grade Road.

Turn left on the FT to go south and return to the Bear Pond trailhead. At 9.9 miles, pass the junction where you began the white-blazed Lower Wekiva Loop Trail. After passing Shelter Camp, cross a bridge and return to the trailhead.

Miles and Directions

0.0   Start at a marked gate/posts near the trailhead kiosk.

0.5   Cross a bridge.

0.7   Pass Shelter Camp and a large tent camping area.

0.8   Come to a Y junction with the start of the white-blazed Lower Wekiva Loop Trail. Go right to join the Lower Wekiva Loop Trail.

3.7   Pass Pine Lily Camp.

5.1   Reach a junction with the yellow-blazed equestrian trail to the FT. (*Option:* Take this trail to cut almost 2 miles from the loop walk.)

6.9   Reach a junction with the main Florida Trail. Follow the orange blazes south for the return.

8.5   Cross East Spur Road.

9.9   Pass the white-blazed trail where you started the Lower Wekiva Loop Trail.

10.7   Arrive back at the Bear Pond south parking lot.

Wekiwa Springs State Park

Wekiwa Springs State Park is a 7,800-acre scenic wonder little changed from the days when the Timucua Indians speared fish in the spring-fed creeks and stalked deer in the uplands. As the metropolitan Orlando area grows ever denser, Wekiwa Springs is becoming a priceless urban preserve of nature. It features extensive hiking with primitive wilderness camping in an otherwise heavily developed part of Central Florida. The nearest town is Apopka, an Indian word apparently meaning "Big Potato."

One of the park system's most popular sites, Wekiwa Springs State Park frequently reaches capacity and may temporarily close for several hours at a time. Its second-magnitude spring gushes 43 million gallons (163 million liters) of crystal-clear water a day into its 0.5-acre swimming hole with a bright sand bottom. The natural swimming pool varies from 1 to 4 feet deep. Simply sitting on the sandy bottom is a popular pastime. Taking a dip in the 72°F spring is the perfect way to finish an overnight hike.

Wekiwa Springs feeds the Wekiva River, designated a National Wild and Scenic River by the National Park Service. It is a popular canoe trail, and the state park has rentals.

Why do the Wekiwa Spring and Wekiva River have different but similar names? Both are Creek Indian words. Wekiwa means "spring of water"; Wekiva translates as "flowing water." Technically, Wekiwa relates to everything in the park where the spring originates, while Wekiva refers to the river and other areas outside the park. Local names don't always follow this distinction. Area streets are known both as Wekiwa and Wekiva. If that seems confusing to you, residents don't know what to make of it either.

Start: Sand Lake parking lot

Distance: 13.5-mile loop; 5.0-mile round-trip to the most remote primitive campsite

Difficulty: Easy to moderate for the primitive campsite hikes; more moderate on the full loop hike

Hiking time: About 5 hours for main trail

Seasons: Nov to mid-May for the most pleasant camping

Fees and permits: Vehicle fee of $6. Primitive camping $5 per person per night; primitive campsites must be reserved in advance through the ranger station.

Trail contact: Wekiwa Springs State Park, 1800 Wekiwa Circle, Apopka 32712; (407) 884-2008; floridastateparks.org/parks-and-trails/wekiwa-springs-state-park

Schedule: Open daily, 8 a.m. to sunset

Dog-friendly: Leashed dogs permitted

Trail surface: Mostly dirt path

Land status: Florida state park

Nearest town: Apopka

Other trail users: Nature watchers

Water availability: It might be possible to get some in the restrooms, but it's far better to bring your own packed and ready to go. Do not drink from the spring without using a filter.

Maps: A good map is unusually important here due to the several overlapping multiuse trails. Beyond the primitive camping area, the main trail intersects an equestrian trail, a

Black bears are common in Central Florida, particularly at Wekiwa Springs State Park. Over-night campers must bear-proof their supplies.

biking trail, and another walking trail. Maps are available at the ranger station or online at floridastateparks.org/sites/default/files/media/file/20190618%20WSSP%20Trail%20Map%20-%20New%20Logo.pdf.

Special considerations: Accessible chairlift and a ramp for spring entry. Four campground sites are accessible. The Wet to Dry Nature Trail is wheelchair accessible. Florida law requires helmets for cyclists age 16 and under. To prevent overcrowding, backpackers must check in at the entrance station like regular campers.

Primitive backpacking sites: Two sites that must be reserved no more than 60 days in advance. Call (407) 884-2008 for the ranger station and also (407) 553-4383. Big Buck Camp is on Rock Springs Run; Camp Cozy is more landlocked. Both have a picnic table, benches, and a firepit with a grill. Both sites can accommodate up to 10 people. You must arrive at the park at least 2 hours before

sunset to make sure you have time to set up before dark.

Camping: The park has 60 developed campsites. Campers who plan to arrive after sunset should call the park on the day of arrival at (407) 553-4383 to get the gate combination and instructions.

Amenities: Campground, restrooms and showers, hiking, paddling, picnicking, snorkeling, swimming, concession, restaurant, equestrian trail, playground, mountain biking, fishing (with Florida license), birding, and more

Cell service: Good

Trail conditions: The hike starts out on relatively even ground and then has some mild descents and ascents. There may be muddy ground approaching Camp Cozy. Depending on recent weather, the loop walk from Camp Cozy to Marker 18 may be a sloppy one. Once the main trail joins the Bicycle Trail at Marker 18, the trail becomes tamer.

36 Wekiwa Springs Loop Trail

Distance: 10.2-mile loop

Finding the trailhead: The park is located about 20 minutes from downtown Orlando. Turn off I-4 at exit 94, then turn left to go under the SR 434 overpass. Follow the "Wekiwa Springs" sign on SR 434 West. Turn right at Wekiwa Springs Road and travel about 4 miles to the park entrance, on the right. After the ranger station, turn left when the entrance road T's. Follow the road until it ends at the Sand Lake parking lot, the starting point for the main trail hike, which also leads to the primitive campsites. Trailhead GPS: 28.722189 / -81.472537

The Hike

Traffic passing the park's main entrance is thick and often continuous. Yet once inside Wekiwa Springs State Park, it's back to the Florida of wading birds, otters, raccoons, alligators, and even Florida black bears. Speaking of bears, you do need to take extra precautions while on the trail and at your campsite. You could possibly encounter a bear on the trail or at a campsite. If that happens, the Florida Park Service advises hikers to talk calmly, stand your ground, and give the bear an exit route. Try to make yourself look larger. Stand your ground, and don't turn your back on the animal. Your greatest bother is likely to be mosquitoes. If camping, bring enough bug repellent to last several days.

Since an overnight hike on the main trail is a major goal, a more detailed description is provided to the primitive campsites. You must arrive at the park 2 hours before sunset to claim your campsite and have time to set up. Whichever campsite you select, keep your food in bear-proof containers to avoid attracting a Florida black bear. It's a rare treat to spot one, but cleaning up after a bear's visit is always messy.

The hike to Big Buck Camp is about 1.5 miles, to Camp Cozy about 2.5 miles. To reach either site, ignore the sequence of numbered trail markers shown on the park map. The shortest direct route to the campsites is by hiking the main trail counterclockwise.

Leaving the Sand Lake parking lot, the hike immediately joins the white-blazed main trail. After passing the edge of Sand Lake, the trail follows a forest road toward Marker 21 on the park hiking map.

The trail leads past towering pines, thick palmettos, and a dense ground covering of ferns. Wildlife is abundant here, so don't be surprised to hear bushes moving or dead palm fronds snapping. Although white-tailed deer and Florida black bear are present, the racket is probably made by nothing more than a lumbering armadillo.

In about 0.3 mile the East–West Cross Trail intersects the main trail. Ignore it and continue straight. Shortly before reaching Marker 21, the trail intersects a forest road that goes directly to Big Buck Camp. Instead, you might want to walk straight ahead and descend to visit Rock Springs Run, an amazingly clear waterway in the dry months.

You may need to push aside some palm fronds to descend to the flowing stream and the jumble of cypress knees lining the bank. If you're here during a rainy period, the normally clear spring run is apt to be discolored by brown tannins.

Hike left along the riverbank for a short distance. Then follow the white blazes as they go left and turn uphill to Big Buck Camp. You now have clocked about 1.5 miles.

Unless you reserved Big Buck Camp, you are now ready to move on to the main trail's second campsite. Camp Cozy is about 1 mile farther on. To get there, you must navigate part of a floodplain that may be muddy, especially in rainy months. Just before Camp Cozy, the landscape becomes a dry upland and the trail meets a forest road. It's a shame the trail cuts right through the camping area.

The Camp Cozy site has a firepit surrounded by benches and a large, mowed place for a tent. A spigot provides unpotable water that must be brought to a rolling boil for 3 minutes before using.

The trail continuing beyond Camp Cozy is marked by several muddy sections. If it's been raining, water levels may be ankle deep in places. The hike is parallel to the floodplain forest of nearby Rock Springs Run and then enters a cypress swamp, so there are many opportunities for wet and muddy feet. Depending on how deep the water is on the trail, this next part of the hike may change from moderate to difficult until the park map's Marker 19.

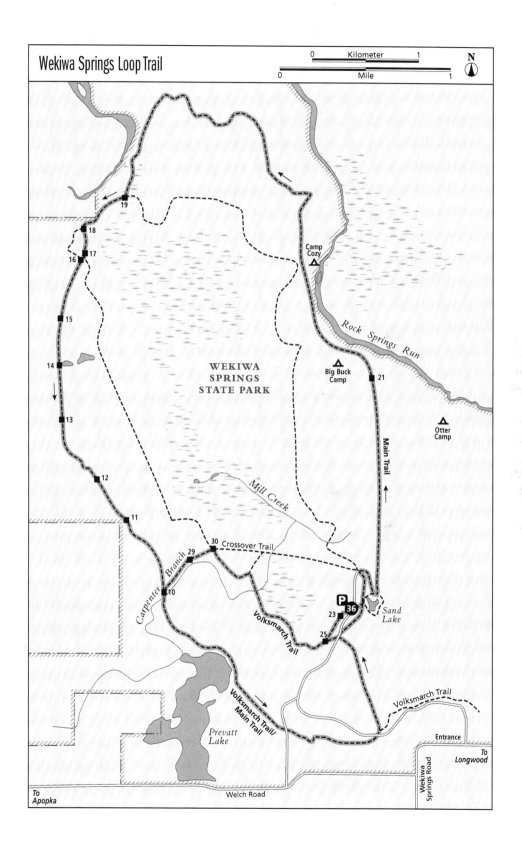

Wekiwa Springs Loop Trail

0   Kilometer   1

0   Mile   1

N

19

18

17

16

15

14

13

12

11

Camp Cozy

WEKIWA SPRINGS STATE PARK

Rock Springs Run

Big Buck Camp

21

Otter Camp

Main Trail

Mill Creek

30   Crossover Trail

29

Carpenter Branch

10

Volksmarch Trail

P 36

23

25

Sand Lake

Volksmarch Trail/ Main Trail

Volksmarch Trail

Prevatt Lake

Entrance

To Longwood

Wekiwa Springs Road

To Apopka

Welch Road

At Marker 19, the trail changes from hikers-only to multiuse, where equestrians have access. You could share the path with them until Marker 18, where they depart and cyclists now have access until Marker 10. As mountain bikes move faster than hikers, be prepared to yield.

From Marker 18 it's possible to make a crossover to Kelly Park/Rock Springs Run, a very scenic place with some of Central Florida's most picturesque landscape.

At Marker 10, when cyclists switch to a different route, hikers using the Volksmarch Trail can access the white-blazed main trail leading back to the Sand Lake trailhead.

Miles and Directions

0.0   Start at the trailhead at the Sand Lake parking area.

0.3   Reach a junction with East-West Cross Trail.

0.8   Reach Marker 21.

1.5   Reach the Big Buck primitive campsite.

2.5   Reach the Camp Cozy primitive campsite.

3.2   Come to a hammock with large and ancient saw palmettos, pines, and oaks.

4.3   Reach a junction with the mountain biking trail.

7.3   At Marker 10, intersect the orange-blazed Volksmarch Trail. (**Option:** If you're ready to return to the trailhead on a shorter path, consider the Volksmarch Trail.)

8.8   Pass a road to a developed campground with potable water.

9.0   Cross paved Park Road.

9.6   Cross a stream on a footbridge.

10.0   Water and restrooms are available here.

10.2   Arrive back at the Sand Lake parking lot.

Lake Kissimmee State Park

Looking like the entrance to a different world, this is the common trailhead for both Lake Kissimmee loop trails.

If you like fishing, hiking could become secondary at 5,930-acre Lake Kissimmee State Park. It is rated one of the of state's top-ten lakes for trophy bass fishing. In Florida, a trophy bass starts at 10 pounds. Numerous high-money fishing tournaments have been held on the lake. A Florida fishing license is required.

Lake Kissimmee State Park is part of the Everglades' headwaters. It is one of Central Florida's top birding areas, with more than 200 species living in or visiting the park. You have the opportunity to see bald eagles, snail kites, sandhill cranes, and possibly even whooping cranes.

The park is also home to fifty species of plants and animals regarded as threatened, of special concern, or endangered. Some of the more common animals to watch for are white-tailed deer, bobcats, turkeys, and bald eagles.

Lake Kissimmee State Park has decided to allow mountain biking on its hiking trails, the kind of hike we've tried to avoid in this guide. Unfortunately, this probably will happen in additional state parks that want their trails to be accessed by as many people as possible. So far it hasn't inconvenienced hikers here, so the hikes remain included. Equestrians use entirely separate trails.

On the Buster Island Loop Trail, expect to encounter a rare breed of free-roaming cattle. They are Florida scrub cattle, descended from the long-horned Andalusian breed imported by the Spanish. Cattle ranching has been a permanent Florida fixture since the founding of St. Augustine in 1565.

Raising cattle became important in Florida during the Civil War, when the state provided beef for Confederate troops. The cattle business became so significant that for many decades, until perhaps 2000, Florida was one of the top-five cattle producers in the county. Theme parks, housing, and wildlife management areas now occupy former cattle range. Florida has slipped to twelfth in the number of beef cows, only about 900,000 animals.

Lake Kissimmee State Park reserves more than 200 acres for raising a herd of scrub cows and horses, just as Florida "Crackers" did in the 1800s. The park's living-history Florida Cow Hunters Camp reenacts those days, with rangers portraying Florida cattlemen on an 1876 cattle drive. They describe what cattlemen's life was like then, including the dangers and challenges they faced before the invention of air-conditioning.

Florida cowpokes were never known as cowboys. Called cattlemen, they became better known as "crackers" due to the sound their whips made as they herded cows. It was the whip's cracking sound, not its lash, that moved the cattle.

Today, Florida claims its own cattle breed called "Florida Crackers," descendants of the cattle the Spanish introduced in the 1500s. They have the same origin as many of the cattle still being raised in Central and South America. Also known as scrub cows, these are animals you may encounter on the Buster Island Loop Trail. They are a hardy, pest-resistant breed colored solid red or a white-gray with black points.

Start: West end of the marina parking lot

Distance: Both loop trails are just under 7 miles.

Difficulty: Easy to moderate, depending how hot it is

Hiking time: 2-3 hours on each hike

Seasons: Mid-Nov to May for cooler and drier weather

Fees and permits: Entry is $5 per vehicle; $2 for pedestrians, bicyclists. Tent and RV camping is $20 per night, plus a $7 RV utility fee for water and electricity. Primitive camping is $5 per night.

Trail contact: Lake Kissimmee State Park, 14248 Camp Mack Rd., Lake Wales 33853; (863) 696-1112; floridastateparks.org/parks-and-trails/lake-kissimmee-state-park

Schedule: Park is open 8 a.m. to sunset. The living history Cow Camp is open from 9:30 a.m. to 4:30 p.m., weekends only, from Oct 1 to May 1, including holidays.

Dog-friendly: Pets must be on a 6-foot leash. Owners must pick up after their pets.

Trail surface: Mostly sand and dirt

Land status: Florida state park

Nearest town: Hesperides

Other trail users: Both loop hikes are also mountain bike trails. You may also encounter nature watchers.

Water availability: Bring your own

Maps: Available at the ranger station

Special considerations: Glamping is available in so-called "luxury pioneer tents" with rugs, a queen bed and linens, end tables with lamps, chandeliers, and an air-conditioning/heat system that makes the inside 5-15 degrees cooler or warmer than the outside. These tents are located near the restrooms. For more information, visit lakekissimmeesp.com/pioneer-tents.

Camping: With both loop trails having a primitive campsite, it's possible to hike a full day and spend the night on one of the trails.

The Cow Camp is a living history re-creation showing what life was like in 1876 for Cracker cattlemen (not cowboys).

Campsites must be reserved in advance. Both campsites can be reserved by individuals, couples, or groups. Maximum capacity is 15 people per campsite. You are required to arrive at the park 3 hours before sundown to make certain you reach your site before dark. The park also has a developed campground with 60 sites.

Amenities: Accessible parking, restrooms, camping, picnic pavilions, and marina. Other activities include horseback riding, fishing, canoeing/kayaking, picnicking, and boating.

Cell service: Generally good but may be spotty in places

Trail conditions: Wet prairie, open forest, scrubby flatwoods, and oak hammocks characterize these trails. Wear sunblock in open areas. Carry insect repellent to discourage ticks as well as mosquitoes. Wildlife is plentiful, so keep your camera ready.

37 Kristin Jacobs Loop Trail

Distance: 6.8-mile loop

Finding the trailhead: *From US 27/Lake Wales*, travel east for 15 miles on SR 60. Turn left (north) onto Boy Scout Road to Camp Mack Road. Turn right onto Camp Mack Road and go 5.5 miles to the park's main entrance

From I-95 on the Atlantic coast, take exit 147 and go west on SR 60. (If you're traveling the Florida Turnpike, a toll road, take exit 163 at Yeehaw Junction and go west on SR 60.) Continue west on SR 60, crossing the Kissimmee River and passing the River Ranch Resort. Turn right

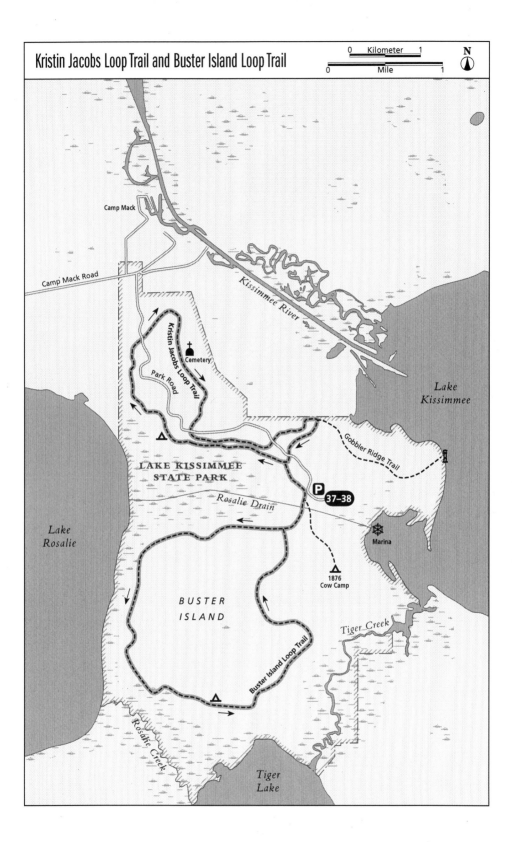

Kristin Jacobs Loop Trail and Buster Island Loop Trail

Kilometer

Mile

N

Camp Mack

Camp Mack Road

Kissimmee River

Kristin Jacobs Loop Trail

Park Road

Cemetery

Lake
Kissimmee

LAKE KISSIMMEE
STATE PARK

Gobbler Ridge Trail

37–38

Rosalie Drain

Marina

Lake
Rosalie

1876
Cow Camp

BUSTER
ISLAND

Tiger Creek

Buster Island Loop Trail

Rosalie Creek

Tiger
Lake

(north) onto Boy Scout Road to Camp Mack Road. Turn right onto Camp Mack Road and go 5.5 miles to the park's main entrance.

Once inside, follow the winding main Park Road to the west end of the marina parking lot. This is where a blue-blazed 0.3-mile access path leads to a large kiosk where the two hikes peel off in different directions. Trailhead GPS: 27.941876 / -81.356913

The Hike

For many years this hike was known simply as the North Loop Trail. The 6.8-mile hike has been renamed in honor of state legislator Kristin Jacobs, who championed environmental issues and spent much of her free time in the park. The hiking path, blazed in yellow, is also used by mountain bikers.

Start the trail clockwise and hike past pines and palmettos as the trail parallels and almost touches the trail you will use for your return hike. The trail then twists to the right and parallels the Park Road, still lost in the distance.

At almost 2 miles, reach a junction with a blue-blazed spur to the primitive campsite located in an oak hammock. It has a picnic table and a fire ring but no water. Continuing, the hike soon reaches the park boundary and then makes a sharp right turn. Soon it's time to cross Park Road, something the trail will do frequently. Wet prairie and open forest mark the trail's next section.

At 3.2 miles, pass a turpentine workers' cemetery. Some of the pine trees in this area have "catface" scars, marking where sap was drained from them. At one time, pine sap was used to waterproof boats and also make turpentine. This extraction process was an important part of the economy in Southern states until as late as the 1960s.

Now the trail begins to have more tree cover and shade. At Marker 7, cross the Park Road and begin the trail paralleling the path you hiked from the marina. The trail crosses the Park Road again at Marker 9. The trail intersects a green-blazed 1.4-mile spur trail that leads to Gobbler Ridge, the shore of Lake Kissimmee, and an observation tower. The name Gobbler Ridge apparently is due to the turkeys frequently seen in the area. The ridge itself is an elevated area believed to have been created by high waves off Lake Kissimmee many years ago.

If you follow the spur to the lake, your total distance for the hike will be about 9.6 miles. To remain on the Kristin Jacobs Loop Trail, cross the Park Road yet again at Marker 13. The hike now intersects the access trail that leads to the parking lot.

Miles and Directions

0.0 Start at west end of the marina parking lot.

0.3 A blue connector trail intersects the yellow-blazed Kristin Jacobs Loop Trail. Go left to make a clockwise hike.

0.4 Cross the Park Road.

1.3 Cross the Park Road again.

1.8 Pass a primitive campsite.

2.1 Cross the Park Road.

3.2	Pass the 1912 turpentine workers' cemetery.
4.5	Cross the Park Road at Marker 7.
5.5	Cross the Park Road at Marker 9.
6.0	Reach a junction with the 1.4-mile Gobbler Ridge trail leading to Lake Kissimmee.
6.5	Intersect the return access trail.
6.8	Arrive back at the parking lot.

38 Buster Island Loop Trail

Distance: 6.9-mile loop

Finding the trailhead: Once inside the park, follow the winding main Park Road to the marina parking lot. A blue-blazed 0.3-mile access path at the west end of the marina parking area leads to a large kiosk where the hikes go off in different directions. Like the Kristin Jacobs Loop Trail, this one is open to mountain bikers. Trailhead GPS: 27.941876 / -81.356913

The Hike

Surrounded by Lake Kissimmee, Lake Rosalie, and Tiger Lake, Buster Island is a genuine island. You'll have this confirmed as the blue-blazed connector trail from the kiosk behind the marina takes you across a bridge and over the Zipprer Canal, which connects Lake Kissimmee with Lake Rosalie.

When the blue-blazed trail intersects the white-blazed Buster Island Loop Trail, start the hike in a counterclockwise direction. This trail borders one of Central Florida's unique dry prairies, an ecosystem that once stretched from coast to coast. Wild grasses, shrubs, and scattered trees are a Florida prairie's main characteristics. Oddly enough, this prairie needs to be burned regularly for it to thrive.

The trail soon moves into open and sunny pine flatwoods. It then moves under an open canopy of widely spaced pine trees and a low understory of scrub oaks and saw palmetto—a type of terrain known as scrubby flatwoods.

After the path leads into an oak hammock and passes a pond, you'll reach the primitive campsite at about 3.5 miles. The site has two picnic tables and two fire rings but no water.

Back on the trail, the hike curves left as you begin your return. The trail enters a dry prairie with a more open landscape. At 6.1 miles, any trace of forest is replaced by open prairie. This is the area where you may spot some Florida Cracker Cattle, with their distinctive semi-long, sharp horns. The animals are nobody's pet and best left alone.

Although Florida Cracker Cattle are one of the oldest breeds in the United States, they are categorized as a very rare breed. They provide beef and milk and are known for their strong muscles, but their meat is also lean and tough, which helps explain why they're not a popular breed.

Once the trail leaves the Buster Island prairie, make the hike back over the bridge and arrive back at the trailhead kiosk at 6.6 miles. Return to the marina via the blue-blazed connector.

Miles and Directions

0.0 Start on the connector trail from the hiking kiosk behind the marina parking lot.

0.3 Join a second blue-blazed connector trail. Cross a bridge and arrive at the white-blazed Buster Island Loop Trail; turn right to follow the loop counterclockwise.

3.5 Leave the flatwoods to enter an oak hammock.

3.7 Arrive at the Buster Island campsite.

4.6 Traverse an oak hammock.

5.0 Hike through a sparse forest.

6.1 Follow the trail to an open prairie.

6.6 Reach a junction with the blue-blazed connector trail at the kiosk.

6.9 Arrive back at the marina parking lot.

Long Haulers

Ocala National Forest

If you plan to use any of the Ocala National Forest facilities before, during, or after your hike, download the Recreation.gov mobile app before arriving at the forest. Ocala campgrounds and recreation areas are cashless. The phone app is advertised as not needing cell service to make and pay for reservations.

The 389,000-acre Ocala National Forest was the first designated national forest east of the Mississippi River. Affectionately known as The Big Scrub, it is the world's largest stand of sand pine scrub forest. It also contains one of the most scenic extensions of the Florida National Scenic Trail, a 75-mile leg that's considered the "crown jewel" of the system.

At some point on a hike here, it's almost a must to leave the trail and swim in one of the freshwater springs in one of the recreation areas. The springs are an essential part of the Ocala experience. Forget about swimming in any of the freshwater lakes along the hike. They are bound to have alligators.

Ocala is the southernmost national forest in the continental United States. It is home to 25 percent of the world's threatened Florida scrub-jay population, contains more than 600 natural lakes and ponds, and protects the world's largest contiguous sand pine scrub forest.

The Ocala Trail is divided into two sections, North and South. Both sections take hikers through rolling sand hills and longleaf pine forests, skirt dozens of ponds, and venture into numerous cypress and gum swamps. Hikers usually have no worry about water-soaked feet thanks to the Florida Trail Association providing boardwalks to span the wet spots.

Be aware this forest is prime black bear habitat. The bears are very interested in your food, not you. A bear bag or bear canister is required for backpackers. Don't leave anything out overnight that isn't sealed.

Unfortunately, the days when you could leave a vehicle at the trailhead and not worry about vandalism or theft are long over. When heading into the woods overnight, it's best to pay a small nightly fee to protect your vehicle inside a recreation area.

The Ocala North and Ocala South Trails are especially popular because they venture into true wilderness and provide many days of relaxed hiking. Another major attraction is the dispersed camping allowed outside of hunting season. Some hikers call this boondocking, but not everywhere is open. The designated locations are large. Some of the most easily accessible places are identified prior to the Ocala North hike description.

The Ocala North Trail usually ends at SR 40. I decided to stop the hike at the Hopkins Prairie Campground, just short of SR 40. This way, both Ocala hikes in this guide have similar lengths. If you prefer to end your Ocala hiking at SR 40, go for it. It's your hike.

The Ocala South Trail traverses 38 miles of mostly pine and hardwood forests on one of Florida's drier hiking routes. The hike begins from the campground at Hopkins Prairie, an open sunny wetland where the birding can be quite good, and wildflowers often brighten the prairie. This trail also takes you close to some of Ocala's best swimming holes and most scenic areas: Alexander Springs and Juniper Springs. Side trails lead to both recreation areas. These are must-stops, if only for a swim and something tastier to eat. Alexander Springs is my longtime favorite—but never on a weekend, when it can be as crowded as a theme park.

If you can find space in your backpack, consider taking a face mask and snorkel to see what's happening in Alexander Springs. Underwater, I once came face-to-face with an otter that suddenly swam up to me, shocking both of us.

Farles Prairie is another must-see and also a rest stop. This huge grassy expanse can be an excellent place for spotting wildlife. You can increase your likelihood of seeing animals by waking early.

Seasons: Mid-Nov to May for the best weather. General gun hunting season lasts from the second week of Nov to the end of the first week of Jan.

Fees and permits: No fees or permits needed for visiting Ocala National Forest or making a thru-hike. Day-use fee of $12 at Juniper Springs, Silver Glen Springs, Wildcat Lake, Clearwater Lake, and the Alexander Springs Recreation Areas. An annual pass is $60 per person or $50 per vehicle. For an updated fee schedule, visit fs.usda.gov/main/florida/passes-permits/recreation.

Trail contact: Lake George District, 17147 E. Hwy. 40, Silver Springs 34488; (352) 625-2520; open weekdays only 7:30 a.m. to 4:00 p.m. Seminole Ranger District, 40929 State Road 19, Umatilla 32784; (352) 669-3153; open weekdays only 7:30 a.m. to 4:30 p.m. Visitor centers in Silver Springs, Salt Springs, and Altoona are open daily, 9 a.m. to 5 p.m., except holidays; fs.fed.us/r8/florida/recreation/index_oca.shtml.

Schedule: The state forest is open 24 hours a day; hunting season is from mid-Nov to mid-Jan, with some access restrictions for nonhunters.

Dog-friendly: Leashed dogs permitted

Trail surface: Dirt path, forest roads, boardwalks

Land status: National forest

Nearest town: Palatka

Other trail users: ATVs, trucks, equestrians on some areas of forest roads

Water availability: Carry enough for your first day and use a water filter for your clean water on the rest of the hike.

Maps: The Florida Trail Association has the best maps. This organization started and built the Florida Trail from the Ocala North and South hikes.

Special considerations: During hunting season, hikers should wear 500 square inches of blaze-orange clothing above the waist, and it must be visible in both front and back. Hunting schedule is available at myfwc.com/hunting/season-dates/. Before making a trip here, check the forest alerts page for temporary closures and other news: fs.usda.gov/alerts/florida/alerts-notices. Rules visitors are expected to follow are outlined here at fs.usda.gov/detail/florida/home/?cid=stelprdb5274793.

Camping: Dispersed camping permits you to camp almost anywhere at no extra charge in specified areas. It is not allowed near a recreation area. Choose a previously used site, pack in your drinking water, and pack out your waste. Camp at least 200 feet from trails/ roads and 100 feet from water sources. Bury human and pet waste at least 6 inches deep and 100 feet from any water source. Minimize campfire impacts by burning wood down to ash, and follow Leave No Trace Principles. Dispersed camping in the woods is allowed in the following areas: Alexander Springs Wilderness, Billie Bay Wilderness, Davenport Landing, Davenport Landing Trail, Juniper Prairie Wilderness, Little Lake George Wilderness,

and the St. Francis Trailhead. A list of the 14 developed campgrounds is available at fs.usda.gov/activity/florida/recreation/ camping-cabins/?recid=70792&actid=29. **Amenities:** More than a dozen developed campgrounds with showers, restrooms, picnic tables, charcoal grills, drinking water, trash receptacles, and sanitation facilities **Cell service:** Should be good, depending on your carrier

39 Ocala North Trail

Start: St. Johns trailhead near the Buckman Lock
Distance: 33.7 miles one way
Difficulty: Easy to moderate, depending on rain and heat
Hiking time: 2–3 days
Trail conditions: The trail grade is easy and dry for the most part. Footbridges or boardwalks

are placed in the wet spots. The trail is worn and well maintained, and road crossings have signage. Heat and humidity become a serious problem for anyone who tackles more distance than they can comfortably handle. The Ocala Trail is intended to be hiked in stages. No need for it to be an endurance contest.

Finding the trailhead: Take SR 19 about 8 miles south of the town of Palatka. Look for a side road that leads to Buckman Lock, part of the old Florida Barge Canal. The address is 210 Buckman Lock Rd., Palatka. The hike starts south of the lock, so its schedule should be irrelevant. Parking and tent camping are available for a fee near the St. Johns trailhead. Trailhead GPS: 29.544255 / -81.728446

The Hike

This 34-mile hike can be broken into several easy day-hike sections, so there is no need to push. Outside of hunting season, you can pitch a tent pretty much anywhere you want if you follow the rules.

After leaving Buckman Lock, the Florida Trail parallels the Cross Florida Barge Canal. At about mile 7, the trail arrives at the spillway of Rodman Dam, built as part of the cross-Florida barge canal project. For decades environmentalists have wanted to remove the dam so the Ocklawaha River can be returned to its natural state. In the meantime, the spillway is a popular place to fish and camp.

Going south from the spillway, the trail passes the Rodman Campground and crosses a variety of forest roads before reaching the Lake Delancy West campground at mile 13.3. The camping area for Florida Trail hikers is 0.3 mile west of the main trail. Campground facilities include water and restrooms. This area also is popular with

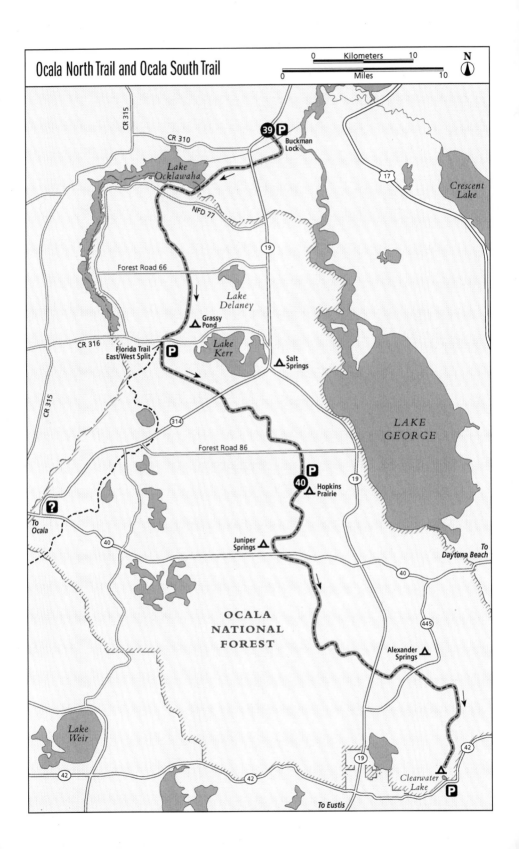

Kilometers 10

0

Miles 10

N

CR 315

CR 310

39 P Buckman Lock

Lake Ocklawaha

NFD 77

17

Crescent Lake

19

Forest Road 66

Lake Delaney

Grassy Pond

CR 316

Florida Trail East/West Split P

Lake Kerr

Salt Springs

CR 315

314

LAKE GEORGE

Forest Road 86

P

40 Hopkins Prairie

19

?

To Ocala

40

Juniper Springs

To Daytona Beach

40

445

OCALA NATIONAL FOREST

Alexander Springs

Lake Weir

42

19

42

Clearwater Lake

P

To Eustis

off-road vehicle riders. Additional campsites are at Grassy Pond (mile 18). It's located on a spur trail and has room for forty sites but no facilities. Grassy Pond is a former forest service campsite now abandoned and with all amenities removed.

Shortly after mile 30, the trail junctions with a 3-mile side trail leading to the Salt Springs Recreation Area, with complete facilities and a natural spring popular with swimmers.

As the main trail continues, it crosses FR 90 and FR 65 and it enters Hopkins Prairie, an interconnected wet and dry prairie landscape surrounded by sand pine and oak scrub. The prairie is a hot spot for birding.

Our Ocala North Trail ends at Hopkins Prairie Campground at mile 33.7. The campground has twenty-one sites and a nightly fee of $12. Check-in time is 2 p.m. and checkout time is 11 a.m. No reservations; this is a first-come, first-served campground.

The campsites are shaded in an oak hammock located on a peninsula surrounded by Hopkins Prairie. Facilities include a hand pump, vault toilet, and posts for hanging lanterns. For more information visit adventureocala.com/hopkins-prairie-campground.

Campground parking is available for campers only. Others must use a trailhead parking area along the campground access road. Anyone wanting to avoid a campground and continue their wilderness experience can use the Juniper Prairie Wilderness Area for dispersed camping. Its northern edge is just 0.3 mile south of Hopkins Prairie Campground. If you want to end the hike at SR 40, continue hiking south another 12 miles.

Miles and Directions

The following mile points are traveled north to south.

- **0.0** Start at the St. Johns trailhead.
- **2.0** Pass SR 19.
- **4.6** Pass the 0.4-mile spur to Rodman Campground.
- **5.4** The Florida Trail enters Ocala National Forest.
- **5.8** Pass stairs leading to the Rodman Spillway.
- **8.1** Cross FR 74.
- **13.3** Pass the Lake Delancy Campground. (**Note:** Water and latrines are available; no electricity.)
- **17.5** Reach a junction with a blue-blazed trail on the right leading to Grassy Pond.
- **19.7** Reach a junction with the Florida Trail's Eastern and Western corridors. This hike describes the Eastern Trail, which goes left.
- **20.1** Reach a junction with a blue-blazed trail coming from the left. The 0.4-mile side trail leads to the 88 Store grocery store, located near Lake Kerr. This is a favorite hiker resupply stop and watering hole.
- **24.0** Pass CR 314, a corridor to the Salt Springs Recreation Area, located 3.4 miles east.
- **24.5** Cross FR 11.

Pine trees and saw palmetto characterize much of the Florida Trail's southern section in Ocala National Forest.

27.1 Pass a connector trail on the left to the Salt Springs Recreation Area.

33.7 Arrive at junction with a blue-blazed trail on the left that leads to the Hopkins Prairie Campground, also the end of our Ocala North hike. The Ocala South hike starts from the campground.

40 Ocala South Trail

Start: Hopkins Prairie Campground
Distance: 38.4 miles one way
Difficulty: Easy to moderate
Hiking time: 2–3 days
Trail conditions: A well-used and well-maintained segment of the Florida Trail, this segment is considered an easy to moderate hike. Although Hopkins Prairie in the northern section is a large wetland open to the sun, many sections are well shaded, but don't stop using sunblock or wearing a hat. The trail passes some heavily used recreation areas where hikers should consider stopping, particularly Alexander Springs and Juniper Springs. Also take time to stop and smell the wildflowers.

Finding the trailhead: The campground at Hopkins Prairie, open seasonally, is the preferred parking area for Florida Trail hikers. From SR 40, go north 9.2 miles on SR 19 and look for the signed turnoff to Hopkins Prairie Road (FR 86). Turn west onto Hopkins Prairie Road and go about 3 miles to FR 86-F, on the right. Turn right onto FR 86-F and go about 1 mile to the campground. Trailhead GPS: 29.275385 / -81.692672

The Hike

Ocala South is easily broken into several easy day-hike sections, so don't feel you have to tackle the rest of the trail in a two-day trek. The distances noted are for Ocala South only; they are not cumulative from Buckman Lock.

The Ocala South hike begins from the Hopkins Prairie Campground. In just 0.6 mile you pass Big Sink, a wide and deep sinkhole that always seems to have water at the bottom. Almost immediately the trail arrives at two important historic Ocala landmarks, located off the main trail. These could consume a day to explore. Research them thoroughly before making this hike.

At 1.8 miles, the trail enters the Juniper Prairie Wilderness Area and intersects the northern trailhead to Pat's Island, one of the forest's most popular historic attractions. Pat's "Island" and other areas like it have a unique significance in the Ocala Forest. A forest island is a landlocked and isolated area of longleaf pines, oaks, and other tall vegetation surrounded by a sea of small scrubby growth.

Pat's Island was named for Patrick Smith, the area's first postmaster, who settled here in the 1840s. The forest service now manages Pat's Island to protect its physical and biological characteristics so it will stay almost exactly as it was almost 200 years ago. Pat's Island is not an area to visit unless you have long pants and long sleeves to protect against biting insects.

Only 0.1 mile farther south, at 1.09 miles, is the northern trailhead for the Yearling Trail. This historic trail pays tribute to author Marjorie Kinnan Rawlings, whose famous novel *The Yearling* was set in the Ocala Forest. Made into a popular movie, the book also won the 1939 Pulitzer Prize. If you're tempted to hike the Yearling Trail, know that the hike is 5.5 miles. Factor this in beforehand and not as a spur-of-the-moment hike unless you have a flexible time frame about where you end the day. You could simply spend another night at Hopkins Prairie.

At 2.5 miles, reach the south junction with both Pat's Island and the Yearling Trails. At 5.3 miles you arrive at Hidden Pond in the Juniper Prairie Wilderness. With no amenities, the pond is still an attractive camping site. It is located on a ridge between a spring-fed pond and a wide wet prairie. A breeze blowing over the wet landscape creates a natural air-conditioning.

Continuing, the trail crosses Whiskey and Whispering Creeks, which may require wading during high water. It then skirts the south edge of Juniper Prairie and at 10.6 miles arrives at the Juniper Springs Recreation Area, one of the two largest campgrounds in Ocala National Forest.

Leaving Juniper Springs Recreation Area, the trail crosses SR 40 and then follows a boardwalk over a stretch of marshland. At mile 18 the trail arrives at Farles Prairie Recreation Area, a huge grassy expanse where camping is no longer permitted due to aggressive bear activity. However, the recreation area still has picnic tables and a vault toilet. East of Farles Prairie is the Pine Castle Bombing Range, where US Navy bombers have held target practice since World War II. It is still an active bombing range, and the unexpected nighttime explosions sometimes awaken terrified campers, who didn't realize there were nighttime bomb drops.

Continuing, the Florida Trail intersects a blue-blazed side trail to the Buck Lake group campsite at 22.6 miles. After crossing a series of forest roads, at 28.4 miles the trail arrives at a blue-blazed 0.5-mile trail leading to the Alexander Springs Recreation Area. Alexander Springs is an outstanding clear freshwater spring well worth viewing from land and also underwater with a mask and snorkel.

To bypass the recreation area camping fee, it's possible to randomly camp in the Alexander Springs Wilderness, a 7,941-acre area extending from Alexander Springs to Lake Dexter.

As the Ocala Trail continues south, it arrives at a very long boardwalk before FR 539, followed by several short ones. At 33.5 miles, the trail goes across a power line right-of-way, then follows a boardwalk over a creek.

After the FT crosses FR 538 and FR 545, you're almost at the hike's end. At 36.9 miles, a 0.4-mile side trail leads to the small unincorporated town of Paisley. Walt's Disney's grandparents are buried in Lake County's Ponceannah Cemetery, located in Paisley. Disney's parents, Flora Call and Elias Disney, were married in Lake County.

Once you bypass Paisley, the trail soon intersects a 0.3-mile blue-blazed trail to Clearwater Lake Campground, the end of your Ocala South hike. Officially, the

Ocala South Trail ends at CR 42, just 0.3 mile east of the campground entrance (GPS: 28.976462 / -81.550256).

Miles and Directions

The following mile points are traveled north to south. The given mileage is not cumulative from the Ocala North section of the Florida Trail.

0.0 Start from the junction with the blue-blazed trail to Hopkins Prairie Campground.

0.6 A large sinkhole with stairs leads to water.

1.8 Arrive at the "Juniper Prairie Wilderness Area SOBO" (southbound) sign, FR 46. Intersect the north trailhead to Pat's Island.

1.9 Arrive at the junction with the Yearling Trail.

2.2 Arrive at the north end the Juniper Prairie Wilderness dispersed camping area.

2.5 Pass the south junction with both the Yearling and Pat's Island Trails.

5.3 Arrive at Hidden Pond, with swimming and primitive camping.

6.8 Cross Whiskey Creek.

7.5 Cross Whispering Creek. (***Note:*** During high water, you may have to wade.)

8.2 Arrive at the south end of the Juniper Prairie Wilderness dispersed camping area.

10.6 Pass the Juniper Springs Recreation Area. (***Note:*** There are developed campsites here.)

12.0 Cross busy SR 40, then follow a boardwalk over marshland.

12.5 Hike the edge of a tallgrass prairie.

18.0 Enjoy a good panoramic view of Farles Prairie.

20.0 Reach a nice spot for dispersed camping.

20.4 Reach the junction with the 0.1-mile blue-blazed trail to Farles Prairie, which offers fishing (with a Florida license) and boating but no camping.

22.6 Reach a junction with the 0.5-mile blue-blazed trail to the Buck Lake group campsite. A separate 1.6-mile hike circles Buck Lake.

25.0 Come to a junction with a SR 19 trailhead.

28.4 Reach a junction with the 0.5-mile blue-blazed trail to Alexander Springs Campground.

28.8 Cross floodplain area with a boardwalk.

32.3 Traverse a long boardwalk, then follow several short ones through another swamp.

33.7 Cross a power line right-of-way, then a boardwalk across a creek.

36.9 A 0.4-mile side trail leads to the town of Paisley.

38.0 Reach a junction with 0.3-mile blue-blazed trail to Clearwater Lake Campground. Since it may cost $34 per person to camp overnight here, consider paying the $12 day-use fee for a hot shower and a chance to clean up before returning home or hiking farther south.

38.4 Arrive at CR 42, the end of your Ocala South hike. The Florida Trail continues through Ocala National Forest toward the Seminole State Forest in the wildlife-rich Wekiva Basin.

Hiker's Checklist

The "best" way to realize the importance of a good checklist is being on a wilderness trail about 15 miles from the trailhead and discovering you forgot an important item. The thing you forgot may be only an inconvenience or a potentially serious problem. A good checklist will help keep you from forgetting the things you need to make your hike safe and enjoyable.

This is only a suggested list. Base your own list on the nature of the hike and your own personal needs. Items will vary depending on whether you are camping near your vehicle or backpacking to more remote campsites and staying out one or more nights. Remember, if you are carrying it on your back, select items judiciously. Weight is a critical factor.

Check each item as you pack.

Day Hike Checklist

- ☐ Polarized sunglasses
- ☐ Waterproof sunblock
- ☐ Insect repellent
- ☐ Hat with full brim
- ☐ Compass and map of hiking area
- ☐ Fanny pack with snacks and two water bottles
- ☐ Cell phone in case of emergency
- ☐ Bandages for blisters
- ☐ Ankle support device in case of sprain
- ☐ First-aid kit with tweezers
- ☐ For thick mosquito country or prolonged sun exposure, lightweight long-sleeved shirt and long pants
- ☐ Dry clothes back at your vehicle in case of rain
- ☐ Ice chest with cold drinks in vehicle for your return

For Extended Hikes

All of the above plus the following items:
- ☐ GPS device
- ☐ Flashlight with spare batteries
- ☐ Water-sterilizing tablets or portable water purifier
- ☐ Body powder for groin and feet
- ☐ Commercial rehydrating salts
- ☐ Antidiarrheal
- ☐ Laxative (we all react differently)
- ☐ Aspirin

Hike Index

THE TEN ESSENTIALS OF HIKING

American Hiking Society

American Hiking Society recommends you pack the "Ten Essentials" every time you head out for a hike. Whether you plan to be gone for a couple of hours or several months, make sure to pack these items. Become familiar with these items and know how to use them. Learn more at **AmericanHiking.org/hiking-resources**

1. Appropriate Footwear

6. Safety Items (light, fire, and a whistle)

2. Navigation

7. First Aid Kit

3. Water (and a way to purify it)

8. Knife or Multi-Tool

4. Food

9. Sun Protection

5. Rain Gear & Dry-Fast Layers

10. Shelter

THE TEN ESSENTIALS OF HIKING

American Hiking Society

American Hiking Society recommends you pack the "Ten Essentials" every time you head out for a hike. Whether you plan to be gone for a couple of hours or several months, make sure to pack these items. Become familiar with these items and know how to use them. Learn more at **AmericanHiking.org/hiking-resources**

1. Appropriate Footwear

6. Safety Items (light, fire, and a whistle)

2. Navigation

7. First Aid Kit

3. Water (and a way to purify it)

8. Knife or Multi-Tool

4. Food

9. Sun Protection

5. Rain Gear & Dry-Fast Layers

10. Shelter